recipes from a
french
kitchen

recipes from a
french
kitchen

**CAROLE CLEMENTS AND
ELIZABETH WOLF-COHEN**

LORENZ BOOKS

This edition published by Lorenz Books in 2001

Published in the USA by Lorenz Books
Anness Publishing Inc.
27 West 20th Street
New York
NY 10011

Lorenz Books is an imprint of Anness Publishing Inc.
www.lorenzbooks.com

Publisher Joanna Lorenz
Managing Editor Linda Fraser
Copy Editor Christine Ingram
Designers Sheila Volpe and Lilian Lindblom
Cover Design Balley Design Associates
Photography and Styling Amanda Heywood
Food Styling Elizabeth Wolf-Cohen assisted by Janet Brinkworth

Front cover: William Lingwood, Photographer;
Helen Trent, Stylist; Sunil Vijayakar, Home Economist

Previously published as *Creative Cooking Library: Taste of France*

1 3 5 7 9 10 8 6 4 2

NOTES

Standard spoon and cup measures are level.

Large eggs are used unless otherwise stated.

CONTENTS

INTRODUCTION

Classic French cooking brings a certain elegance to a meal. It creates a sense of occasion that makes any gathering festive. Even though the food itself may be quite simple, that distinctive French style makes it special – whether it is something just for the two of you or a formal dinner for eight.

The recipes in this book are suitable for all kinds of gatherings. Perfect for home entertaining, many of them can be prepared ahead or require only minimal last-minute attention. Our simple step-by-step format makes it easy to master the basics of French cooking and present your food with French flair.

These recipes have been streamlined as much as possible in response to the time constraints of today's busy cook. Many lend themselves to advance preparation, including nearly all of the desserts and first courses, or reheat readily. There is plenty of helpful advice for entertaining and clever tips, such as keeping a fragile sauce hot in a Thermos container. Most of the recipes serve for four, six or eight people; some are designed for a romantic twosome.

The French style of serving a meal in separate courses provides the opportunity to savor each dish and allows time for leisurely conversation. A casual lunch or supper might be only two courses, but more formal occasions are often celebrated with a meal of three or four courses. Obviously, with several courses, the portions should be moderate, so guests will still have room for dessert.

Menu selection is one of the keys to successful entertaining. A manageable menu makes the difference between a relaxed host or hostess and a frazzled one. Choose at least one course which can be prepared completely in advance, such as a cold first course or a soup that needs only reheating. A frozen dessert is ideal – in fact, most of the desserts in this book lend themselves to advance preparation. Limit yourself to only one dish that needs last-minute attention. Even then, chopping, measuring or trimming can usually be done ahead.

In planning a menu, give some thought to balancing the courses between substantial and light, rich and refreshing. There are physical considerations, too, such as your oven size and preparation space, crockery and cutlery supply and seating capacity.

Careful planning can eliminate much of the stress of home entertaining and, more important, it can enable you to enjoy your own party. This is especially true when the cook has limited time available on the day of the event.

Decide what can be done ahead and do it. Polishing candle holders, ironing table linens and general

Chicken liver mousse is an ideal first course for entertaining. Not only does it look and taste impressive, but it can be prepared completely in advance and chilled until needed.

Sorting out flowers, crockery, glasses and cutlery can be done ahead, giving you less to worry about on-the day of your party.

housecleaning should be done well in advance. Arranging fresh flowers, shopping and preparing some of the food can certainly be done at least one day ahead. Indeed, some dishes are actually improved by a day or two in the refrigerator. On the day of the party, get out all the dishes you will need for each course, including serving dishes, dessert plates and coffee cups. You may need to use a trolley or set up an additional table to facilitate serving.

Organize the cooking so that everything possible can be completed well before guests are due to arrive. Many recipes can be prepared in stages, following a recipe to the point of finishing the sauce, for instance, then later reheating to that point before completing the recipe. Take

advantage of your appliances: rice or mashed potatoes cooked earlier in the day reheat beautifully in a microwave or in a casserole in a conventional oven. Give some thought to safety, however, and chill food that is cooked more than an hour or so ahead. If using a microwave oven, follow manufacturer's guidelines to make sure food is thoroughly reheated.

When entertaining alone, you may wish to ask a friend to help with serving, pour wine or keep conversation going while you are away from the table. If you entertain often, it is a good idea to keep a record of what you served to whom, so they don't get the same spectacular dessert three times in a row (but if they do, they probably won't mind).

The classic French recipes in this book create a party atmosphere

almost on their own, bringing French flair to your table. We guide you every step of the way, so you can bask in the success of gracious home entertaining in classic French style.

Tips for the Beginner:
● Practice makes perfect – the more often you entertain, the easier it becomes. Invite just two or three good friends over for informal gatherings before you tackle dinner for the boss or a New Year's Eve party. Don't be too ambitious at first – and have a good time yourself!
● Simplify the menu. Homemade soup, good bread and a do-ahead dessert make a great lunch or supper. Add a cheese course and green salad if you are afraid people won't have enough to eat (this is usually an unfounded fear).
● Choose a menu of all make-ahead recipes or consider serving one course that needs no preparation – smoked salmon to start or a bowl of fresh strawberries for dessert.
● Use a timer to help remember when things need attention. When you are pouring apéritifs or eating the first course, don't leave the timing of the dish that is cooking in the oven to chance.

SOUPS
AND
FIRST
COURSES

The French almost always serve a first course,
even for casual family meals, and soup is often
chosen. It provides a satisfying beginning to the
meal – either as a light prelude to a more
substantial main course or partnered with a
gratin or egg dish for a traditional supper.
Other first courses may be more elaborate,
especially for celebrations, but many, such as
terrines and mousses, can be made ahead.
Serving a first course, however simple it may
be, makes a meal memorable.

SAFFRON MUSSEL SOUP

Soupe de Moules Safranée

This is one of France's most delicious seafood soups — for day-to-day eating, the French would normally serve all the mussels in their shells. Serve with plenty of French bread.

SERVES 4–6

3 tbsp unsalted butter
8 shallots, finely chopped
1 bouquet garni
1 tsp black peppercorns
1½ cups dry white wine
2¼ pounds mussels, scrubbed and debearded
2 medium leeks, trimmed and finely chopped
1 fennel bulb, finely chopped
1 carrot, finely chopped
several saffron strands
4 cups fish or chicken broth
½ cup whipping cream
2–3 tbsp cornstarch, blended with 3 tbsp cold water
½ cup whipping cream
1 medium tomato, peeled, seeded and finely chopped
2 tbsp Pernod (optional)
salt and freshly ground black pepper

1 ▲ In a large heavy pan, melt half the butter over a medium-high heat. Add half the shallots and cook for 1–2 minutes until softened but not colored. Add the bouquet garni, peppercorns and white wine and bring to a boil. Add the mussels, cover tightly and cook over a high heat for 3–5 minutes, shaking the pan occasionally, until the mussels have opened.

2 With a slotted spoon, transfer the mussels to a bowl. Strain the liquid through a cheesecloth-lined strainer and reserve.

3 ▲ When the mussel shells are cool enough to handle, pull open and remove most of the mussels, adding any extra juices to the reserved liquid. Discard any closed mussels.

4 Rinse the saucepan and melt the remaining butter over medium heat. Add the remaining shallots and cook for 1–2 minutes. Add the leeks, fennel, carrot and saffron and cook for 3–5 minutes until softened.

5 Stir in the reserved cooking liquid, bring to a boil and cook for 5 minutes until the vegetables are tender and the liquid is slightly reduced. Add the broth and bring to a boil, skimming any foam that rises to the surface. Season with salt, if needed, and black pepper and cook for 5 minutes more.

6 ▲ Stir the blended cornstarch into the soup. Simmer for 2–3 minutes until the soup is slightly thickened, then add the cream, mussels and chopped tomato. Stir in Pernod, if using, and cook for 1–2 minutes until hot, then serve at once.

SHRIMP BISQUE

Bisque de Crevettes

The classic French method for making a bisque requires pushing the shellfish through a tamis, *or drum sieve. This is much simpler and the result is just as smooth.*

SERVES 6–8

1½ pounds small or medium cooked shrimp in the shell
1½ tbsp vegetable oil
2 onions, halved and sliced
1 large carrot, sliced
2 celery stalks, sliced
8 cups water
a few drops of lemon juice
2 tbsp tomato paste
bouquet garni
4 tbsp butter
⅓ cup flour
3–4 tbsp brandy
⅔ cup whipping cream
salt and white pepper

1 Remove the heads from the shrimp and peel away the shells, reserving the heads and shells for the stock. Chill the peeled shrimp.

2 ▲ Heat the oil in a large saucepan, add the shrimp heads and shells and cook over high heat, stirring frequently, until they start to brown. Reduce the heat to medium, add the onions, carrot and celery and fry gently, stirring occasionally, for about 5 minutes until the onions start to soften.

3 Add the water, lemon juice, tomato paste and bouquet garni. Bring the broth to a boil, then reduce the heat, cover and simmer gently for 25 minutes. Strain the broth through a sieve.

4 ▼ Melt the butter in a heavy saucepan over medium heat. Stir in the flour and cook until just golden, stirring occasionally. Add the brandy and gradually pour in about half of the shrimp broth, whisking vigorously until smooth, then whisk in the remaining liquid. Season with salt, if necessary, and white pepper. Reduce the heat, cover and simmer for 5 minutes, stirring frequently.

5 ▲ Strain the soup into a clean saucepan. Add the cream and a little extra lemon juice to taste, then stir in most of the reserved shrimp and cook over medium heat, stirring frequently, until hot. Serve at once garnished with the reserved shrimp.

COLD LEEK AND POTATO SOUP

Vichyssoise

Serve this flavorful soup with a dollop of crème fraîche or sour cream and sprinkle with a few snipped fresh chives – or, on very special occasions, garnish with a small spoonful of caviar.

SERVES 6–8

1 pound potatoes (about 3 large),
   peeled and cubed
6 cups chicken broth
4 medium leeks, trimmed
⅔ cup crème fraîche or
   sour cream
salt and freshly ground black pepper
3 tbsp chopped fresh chives,
   to garnish

1 Put the potatoes and broth in a saucepan or flameproof casserole and bring to a boil. Reduce the heat and simmer for 15–20 minutes.

2 ▼ Make a slit along the length of each leek and rinse well under cold running water. Slice thinly.

3 ▲ When the potatoes are barely tender, stir in the leeks. Season with salt and pepper and simmer for 10–15 minutes until the vegetables are soft, stirring occasionally. If the soup appears too thick, thin it down with a little more broth or water.

4 ▲ Purée the soup in a blender or food processor, in batches if necessary. If you would prefer a very smooth soup, pass it through a food mill or press through a coarse sieve. Stir in most of the cream, cool and then chill. To serve, ladle into chilled bowls and garnish with a swirl of cream and chopped chives.

VARIATION

To make a low-fat soup, use low-fat sour cream. Alternatively, leave out the cream altogether and thin the soup with a little skim milk.

WILD MUSHROOM SOUP   *Velouté de Champignons Sauvages*

In France, many people pick their own wild mushrooms, taking them to a pharmacist to be checked before using them in all sorts of delicious dishes. The dried mushrooms bring an earthy flavor to this soup, but use 6 ounces fresh wild mushrooms instead when available.

SERVES 6–8

1 ounce dried wild mushrooms, such as morels, cèpes or porcini
6 cups chicken broth
2 tbsp butter
2 onions, coarsely chopped
2 garlic cloves, chopped
2 pounds button or other cultivated mushrooms, trimmed and sliced
½ tsp dried thyme
¼ tsp ground nutmeg
2–3 tbsp flour
½ cup Madeira or dry sherry
½ cup crème fraîche or sour cream
salt and freshly ground black pepper
snipped fresh chives, to garnish

1 ▲ Put the dried mushrooms in a strainer and rinse well under cold running water, shaking to remove as much sand as possible. Place them in a saucepan with 1 cup of the broth and bring to a boil over medium-high heat. Remove the pan from the heat and set aside for 30–40 minutes to soak.

COOK'S TIP

Serve the soup with a little extra cream swirled on top, if you like.

2 Meanwhile, in a large heavy saucepan or flameproof casserole, melt the butter over medium-high heat. Add the onions and cook for 5–7 minutes until they are well softened and just golden.

3 ▲ Stir in the garlic and fresh mushrooms and cook for 4–5 minutes until they begin to soften, then add the salt and pepper, thyme and nutmeg and sprinkle over the flour. Cook for 3–5 minutes, stirring frequently, until blended.

4 ▲ Add the Madeira or sherry, the remaining chicken broth, the dried mushrooms and their soaking liquid and cook, covered, over medium heat for 30–40 minutes until the mushrooms are very tender.

5 Purée the soup in batches in a blender or food processor. Strain it back into the saucepan, pressing firmly to force the purée through the sieve. Stir in the crème fraîche or sour cream and sprinkle with the snipped chives just before serving.

BROILED GOAT CHEESE SALAD

Salade de Chèvre

Here is the salad and cheese course on one plate – or serve it as a quick and satisfying first course or light lunch. The fresh tangy flavor of goat cheese contrasts with the mild salad leaves.

SERVES 4

2 firm round whole goat cheeses, such as Crottin de Chavignol *or* Coach Farm Chèvre *(about 2½–4 ounces each)*
4 slices French bread
extra virgin olive oil, for drizzling
5–6 cups mixed salad leaves
chopped fresh chives, to garnish
FOR THE VINAIGRETTE DRESSING
½ garlic clove
1 tsp Dijon mustard
1 tsp white wine vinegar
1 tsp dry white wine
3 tbsp extra virgin olive oil
salt and freshly ground black pepper

1 ▼ To make the dressing, rub a large salad bowl with the cut side of the garlic clove. Combine the mustard, vinegar and wine, salt and pepper in the bowl. Whisk in the olive oil, 1 tbsp at a time, to form a thick vinaigrette.

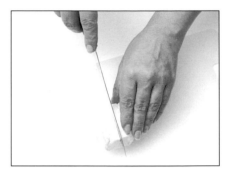

2 ▲ Cut the goat cheeses in half crosswise using a sharp knife.

3 ▲ Preheat the broiler. Arrange the bread slices on a baking sheet and toast the bread on one side. Turn over and place a piece of cheese, cut side up, on each slice. Drizzle with olive oil and broil until the cheese is lightly browned.

4 ▲ Add the greens to the salad bowl and toss to coat them with the dressing. Divide the salad among four plates, top each with a goat cheese croûton and serve, garnished with chives.

CURLY ENDIVE SALAD WITH BACON *Frisée aux Lardons*

This country-style salad is popular all over France. When they are in season, dandelion leaves often replace the endive and the salad is sometimes sprinkled with chopped hard-boiled egg.

SERVES 4

6 cups curly endive or escarole leaves
5–6 tbsp extra virgin olive oil
6 ounce piece of smoked bacon, diced, or
   6 thick-cut bacon slices, cut crosswise
   into thin strips
1 cup white bread cubes
1 small garlic clove, finely chopped
1 tbsp red wine vinegar
2 tsp Dijon mustard
salt and freshly ground black pepper

1 ▲ Tear the lettuce into bite-size pieces and put in a salad bowl.

2 ▲ Heat 1 tbsp of the oil in a medium non-stick frying pan over a medium-low heat and add the bacon. Fry gently until well browned, stirring occasionally. Remove the bacon with a slotted spoon and drain on paper towels.

3 ▼ Add another 2 tbsp of oil to the pan and fry the bread cubes over medium-high heat, turning frequently, until evenly browned. Remove the bread cubes with a slotted spoon and drain on paper towels. Discard any remaining fat.

4 ▲ Stir the garlic, vinegar and mustard into the pan with the remaining oil and heat until just warm, whisking to combine. Season to taste, then pour the dressing over the salad and sprinkle with the fried bacon and croûtons.

SEAFOOD IN PUFF PASTRY

Feuilletés aux Fruits de Mer

This classic combination of seafood in a creamy sauce served in a puff pastry case is found as an appetizer on the menus of many elegant restaurants in France.

SERVES 6

12 ounces puff pastry
1 egg beaten with 1 tbsp water,
    to glaze
4 tbsp dry white wine
2 shallots, finely chopped
1 pound mussels, scrubbed and debearded
1 tbsp butter
1 pound sea scallops, cut in half
    crosswise
1 pound raw shrimp, peeled
6 ounces cooked lobster meat, sliced
FOR THE SAUCE
1 cup unsalted butter, diced
2 shallots, finely chopped
1 cup fish stock
6 tbsp dry white wine
1–2 tbsp cream
lemon juice
salt and white pepper
fresh dill sprigs, to garnish

1 ▼ Lightly grease a large baking sheet and sprinkle with a little water. On a lightly floured surface, roll out the pastry into a rectangle slightly less than ¼ inch thick. Using a sharp knife, cut into six diamond shapes about 5 inches long. Transfer to the baking sheet. Brush pastry with egg glaze. Using the tip of a knife, score a line ½ inch from the edge, then lightly mark the center in a criss-cross pattern.

2 Chill the pastry for 30 minutes. Preheat the oven to 425°F. Bake for about 20 minutes until puffed and brown. Transfer to a wire rack and, while still hot, remove each lid, cutting along the scored line to free it. Scoop out any uncooked dough from the bases and discard, then leave the pastry to cool completely.

3 In a large saucepan, bring the dry white wine and shallots to a boil over a high heat. Add the mussels to the pan and cook, tightly covered, for 4–6 minutes until the shells open, shaking the pan occasionally. Remove any mussels that do not open. Reserve six mussels for the garnish, then remove the rest from their shells and set aside in a bowl, covered. Strain the cooking liquid through a cheesecloth-lined strainer and reserve for the sauce.

4 ▲ In a heavy frying pan, melt the butter over medium heat. Add the scallops and shrimp, cover tightly and cook for 3–4 minutes, shaking and stirring occasionally, until they feel just firm to the touch; do not overcook.

5 Using a slotted spoon, transfer the scallops and shrimp to the bowl with the mussels and add any cooking juices to the mussel liquid.

6 ▲ To make the sauce, melt 2 tbsp of the butter in a heavy saucepan. Add the shallots and cook for 2 minutes. Pour in the fish stock and boil for about 15 minutes over high heat until reduced by three-quarters. Add the white wine and reserved mussel liquid and boil for 5–7 minutes until reduced by half. Lower the heat to medium and whisk in the remaining butter, a little at a time, to make a smooth thick sauce (lift the pan from the heat if the sauce begins to boil). Whisk in the cream and season with salt, if needed, pepper and lemon juice. Keep warm over very low heat, stirring frequently.

7 Warm the pastry bases in a warm oven for about 10 minutes. Put the mussels, scallops and shrimp in a large saucepan. Stir in a quarter of the sauce and reheat gently over low heat. Gently stir in the lobster meat and cook for 1 minute more.

8 Arrange the pastry bases on individual plates. Divide the seafood mixture equally among them and top with the lids. Garnish each with a mussel and a dill sprig and spoon the remaining sauce around the edges or serve separately.

FISH TERRINE

Terrine de Poisson

This colorful layered terrine makes a spectacular presentation for a special occasion. It is typical of those found in the best charcuteries in France and great for entertaining since it is prepared ahead.

<u>SERVES 6</u>

1 pound skinless white fish fillets
8–10 ounces thinly sliced smoked salmon
2 cold egg whites
¼ tsp each salt and white pepper
pinch of ground nutmeg
1 cup heavy cream
2 cups (packed) small tender spinach leaves
lemon mayonnaise, to serve

1 Cut the white fish fillets into 1 inch pieces, removing any bones as you work. Spread out the fish pieces on a plate, cover with plastic wrap. Place in the freezer for about 15 minutes until very cold.

2 ▲ Lightly grease a 5 cup terrine or loaf pan and line the base with nonstick baking paper, then line the base and sides of the pan with smoked salmon slices, letting them overhang the edge. Preheat the oven to 350°F.

3 Remove the fish from the freezer, then process in a food processor until it is a very smooth purée, stopping the machine and scraping down the sides two or three times.

4 Add the egg whites, one at a time, then add the salt, pepper and nutmeg. With the machine running, pour in the cream and stop as soon as it is blended. (If overprocessed, the cream will thicken too much.)

5 Transfer the fish mixture to a large glass bowl. Put the spinach leaves into the food processor and purée. Add one-third of the fish mixture to the spinach and process until just combined, scraping down the sides once or twice.

6 ▲ Spread half the plain fish mixture in the base of the pan and smooth it level. Spoon the green fish mixture over the top and smooth the surface, then cover with the remaining plain mixture and smooth the top. Fold the overhanging pieces of salmon over the top to enclose the mixture. Tap the pan to settle the mixture and remove any air pockets, then cover the terrine with a double layer of foil.

7 Put the terrine in a roasting pan and pour in enough boiling water to come halfway up the sides of the terrine. Bake for about 1 hour, until a skewer inserted in the center comes out clean. Allow to cool, wrap well and chill until firm or overnight.

8 To serve the terrine, turn out onto a board and slice. Arrange slices on individual plates and serve with lemon mayonnaise.

BREADED SOLE BATONS

Goujonettes de Sole

Goujons are tiny fish that are fried until crisp and eaten whole. In this dish, sole fillets are cut into strips that, when cooked, resemble goujons. *The French even bring a sense of style to fish fingers!*

SERVES 4

*10 ounces lemon sole fillets,
    skinned
2 eggs
1½ cups fine fresh breadcrumbs
6 tbsp flour
salt and freshly ground black pepper
vegetable oil, for frying
tartar sauce and lemon, to serve*

1 ▲ Cut the fish fillets into long diagonal strips about ¾ inch wide.

2 ▲ Break the eggs into a shallow dish and beat well with a fork. Place the breadcrumbs in another shallow dish. Put the flour in a large plastic bag and season with salt and freshly ground black pepper.

3 ▼ Dip the fish strips in the egg, turning to coat well. Place on a plate and then taking a few at a time, shake them in the bag of flour. Dip the fish strips in the egg again and then in the breadcrumbs, turning to coat well. Place on a tray in a single layer, not touching. Let the coating set for at least 10 minutes.

4 ▲ Heat ⅜ inch oil in a large frying pan over medium-high heat. When the oil is hot (a cube of bread will sizzle) fry the fish strips for about 2–2½ minutes in batches, turning once, taking care not to overcrowd the pan. Drain on paper towels and keep warm. Serve the fish with tartar sauce and lemon.

CHICKEN LIVER MOUSSE *Mousse de Foie de Volaille*

This mousse makes an elegant yet easy first course. The onion marmalade makes a delicious accompaniment, along with a salad of chicory or other bitter leaves.

SERVES 6–8

1 pound chicken livers
¾ cup butter, diced
1 small onion, finely chopped
l garlic clove, finely chopped
½ tsp dried thyme
2–3 tbsp brandy
salt and freshly ground black pepper
green salad, to serve

FOR THE ONION MARMALADE
2 tbsp butter
1 pound red onions, thinly sliced
1 garlic clove, finely chopped
½ tsp dried thyme
2–3 tbsp raspberry or red wine vinegar
1–2 tbsp clear honey
¼ cup raisins

1 Trim the chicken livers, cutting off any green spots and removing any filaments or fat.

2 ▲ In a heavy frying pan, melt 2 tbsp of the butter over a medium heat. Add the onion and cook for 5–7 minutes until soft and golden, then add the garlic and cook for 1 minute more. Increase the heat to medium-high and add the chicken livers, thyme, salt and pepper. Cook for 3–5 minutes until the livers are colored, stirring frequently; the livers should remain pink inside, but not raw. Add the brandy and cook for 1 minute more.

3 ▲ Using a slotted spoon, transfer the livers to a food processor fitted with the metal blade. Pour in the cooking juices and process for 1 minute, or until smooth, scraping down the sides once. With the machine running, add the remaining butter, a few pieces at a time, until it is incorporated.

4 ▲ Press the mousse mixture through a fine sieve with a wooden spoon or rubber spatula.

COOK'S TIP

The mousse will keep for 3–4 days. If made ahead, cover and chill until ready to use. The onion marmalade can be made up to 2 days ahead and gently reheated over a low heat or in the microwave until just warm.

5 ▲ Line a 2 cup loaf pan with plastic wrap, smoothing out as many wrinkles as possible. Carefully pour the mousse mixture into the lined pan. Cool, then cover and chill until firm, or overnight.

6 ▲ To make the onion marmalade, heat the butter in a heavy frying pan over medium-low heat, add the onions and cook for 20 minutes until softened and just colored, stirring frequently. Stir in the garlic, thyme, vinegar, honey and raisins and cook, covered, for 10–15 minutes until the onions are completely soft and jam-like, stirring occasionally. Spoon into a bowl and cool to room temperature.

7 ▲ To serve, dip the loaf pan into hot water for 5 seconds, wipe dry and invert onto a board. Lift off the pan, peel off the plastic wrap and smooth the surface with a knife. Serve sliced with a little of the onion marmalade and a green salad.

EGGS
AND
CHEESE

The French way with eggs and cheese always creates a sense of occasion. A cheese board can provide a novel alternative to dessert or precede it. Offered after the main course, cheese is often accompanied by a green salad. Elegant egg dishes – baked in ramekins or softly scrambled, for instance – are usually served as a first course in France, but can also be enjoyed for brunch or as a light lunch. Classic French cooking celebrates the versatility of eggs and cheese.

SCRAMBLED EGGS WITH PEPPERS *Pipérade à la Basquaise*

This dish comes from the Basque country in the Pyrenees, piper *being Basquaise for pepper.*

SERVES 4

*4 tbsp bacon fat, duck fat or
    olive oil
2 onions, coarsely chopped
3 or 4 green or red bell peppers
    (or mixed), cored and chopped
2 garlic cloves, finely chopped
small pinch of chili powder or cayenne
    pepper, to taste
2 pounds ripe tomatoes, peeled, seeded
    and chopped
½ tsp dried oregano or thyme
8 eggs, lightly beaten
salt and freshly ground black pepper
chopped fresh parsley, to garnish*

1 Heat the fat or oil in a large heavy frying pan over medium-low heat. Add the onions and cook, stirring occasionally, for 5–7 minutes until they are softened but not browned.

2 ▲ Stir in the peppers, garlic and chili powder or cayenne. Cook for 5 minutes more until the peppers soften, stirring frequently.

COOK'S TIP

Make sure that you cook the peppers until the pan is almost completely dry before adding the eggs, otherwise the finished dish will be too wet.

---

3 Stir in the tomatoes and season with salt and pepper and the oregano or thyme. Cook over medium heat for 15–20 minutes until the peppers are soft, the liquid has evaporated and the mixture is thick. Stir occasionally to prevent the mixture burning and sticking to the pan.

4 ▲ Add the beaten eggs to the vegetables and stir over low heat for 5–8 minutes until the mixture is thickened and softly set. Scatter over the parsley and serve.

SCRAMBLED EGGS WITH CAVIAR *Oeufs Brouillés au Caviar*

In France, scrambled eggs are cooked slowly so they are smooth and rich – creamy and never dry.

SERVES 4

*3 tbsp butter, cut into small pieces
8 eggs, plus 1 egg yolk
1 tbsp crème fraîche, sour cream or heavy
    cream
1–2 tbsp chopped fresh chives
4 slices lightly toasted brioche, buttered,
    plus more to serve
2 ounces caviar
salt and white pepper
chopped fresh chives, to garnish*

1 In a large heavy frying pan or saucepan, melt half the butter over medium-low heat.

2 ▲ Beat the eggs and egg yolk well and season with salt and pepper. Pour into the pan and cook gently, stirring constantly until the mixture begins to thicken and set; this may take 10–12 minutes or longer. Gradually stir in the remaining butter, lifting the pan from the heat occasionally to slow the cooking.

3 ▼ When the eggs are just set, take the pan off the heat and stir in the cream and chives. Arrange the buttered brioche slices on plates and divide the scrambled egg among them. Top each serving with a spoonful of caviar. Garnish with chives and serve with extra toasted brioche.

POACHED EGGS WITH SPINACH   *Oeufs Pochés à la Florentine*

This classic recipe may be served as a first course, but is also excellent for a light lunch or brunch.

SERVES 4

2 tbsp butter
1 pound young spinach leaves
½ tsp vinegar
4 eggs
salt and freshly ground black pepper
FOR THE HOLLANDAISE SAUCE
¾ cup butter, cut into pieces
2 egg yolks
1 tbsp lemon juice
1 tbsp water
salt and white pepper

COOK'S TIP

Hollandaise sauce is quick and easy to make in a blender or food processor. If you wish, you can make it an hour or two in advance and keep it warm in a wide-mouthed Thermos.

---

1 To make the hollandaise sauce, melt the butter in a small saucepan over medium heat until it bubbles, then remove from the heat.

2 ▲ Put the egg yolks, lemon juice and water into a blender or food processor and blend. With the machine running, slowly pour in the hot butter in a thin stream. Stop pouring when you reach the milky solids at the bottom. Season with salt and pepper and more lemon juice if needed. Transfer to a serving bowl, cover and keep warm.

3 ▲ Melt the butter in a heavy frying pan or saucepan over a medium heat. Add the spinach and cook until wilted, stirring occasionally. Season and keep warm.

4 ▲ To poach the eggs, bring a medium pan of lightly salted water to a boil and add the vinegar. Break an egg into a saucer and slide the egg into the water. Reduce the heat and simmer for a few minutes until the white is set and the yolk is still soft. Remove with a slotted spoon and drain. Trim any rough edges with scissors and keep warm. Cook the remaining eggs in the same way.

5 To serve, spoon the spinach on to warmed plates and make an indentation in each mound. Place the eggs on top and pour over a little hollandaise sauce.

BAKED EGGS WITH CREAMY LEEKS *Oeufs en Cocotte aux Poireaux*

The French have traditionally enjoyed eggs prepared in many different ways. Vary this simple yet elegant dish by using other vegetables, such as puréed spinach, or ratatouille, as a base.

SERVES 4

1 tbsp butter, plus extra for greasing
½ pound small leeks, thinly sliced
    (about 2 cups)
5–6 tbsp heavy cream
ground nutmeg
4 eggs
salt and freshly ground black pepper

1 ▲ Preheat the oven to 375°F. Generously butter the base and sides of four small ramekins or individual soufflé dishes.

2 ▲ Melt the butter in a small frying pan and cook the leeks over medium heat, stirring frequently, until softened but not browned.

3 ▼ Add 3 tbsp of the cream and cook gently for about 5 minutes until the leeks are very soft and the cream has thickened a little. Season with salt, pepper and nutmeg.

VARIATION

For an even quicker dish, put 1 tbsp of cream in each dish with some chopped herbs. Break in the eggs, add 1 tbsp cream and a little grated cheese, then bake.

4 ▲ Arrange the ramekins in a shallow baking dish and divide the leeks among them. Break an egg into each, spoon 1–2 tsp of the remaining cream over each egg and season lightly.

5 Pour boiling water into the baking dish to come halfway up the sides of the ramekins or soufflé dishes. Bake for about 10 minutes, until the whites are set and the yolks are still soft, or a little longer if you prefer them more well done.

PROVENÇAL SWISS CHARD OMELETTE

Trouchia

This traditional flat omelette can also be made with fresh spinach, but Swiss chard leaves are typical in Provence. It is delicious served with small black Niçoise olives.

SERVES 6

1½ pounds Swiss chard leaves without stalks
4 tbsp olive oil
1 large onion, sliced
5 eggs
salt and freshly ground black pepper

1 Wash the Swiss chard well in several changes of water and pat dry. Stack four or five leaves at a time and slice across into thin ribbons. Steam the chard until wilted, then drain in a strainer and press out any liquid with the back of a spoon.

2 ▼ Heat 2 tbsp of the olive oil in a large frying pan. Add the onion and cook over medium-low heat for about 10 minutes until soft, stirring occasionally. Add the chard and cook for 2–4 minutes more until the leaves are tender.

3 ▲ In a large bowl, beat the eggs and season with salt and pepper, then stir in the cooked vegetables.

4 Heat the remaining 2 tbsp of oil in a large non-stick frying pan over medium-high heat. Pour in the egg mixture and reduce the heat to medium-low. Cook the omelette, covered, for 5–7 minutes until the egg mixture is set around the edges and almost set on top.

5 ▲ To turn the omelette over, loosen the edges and slide it onto a large plate. Place the frying pan over the omelette and, holding them tightly, carefully invert the pan and plate together. Lift off the plate and continue cooking for 2–3 minutes more. Slide the omelette onto a serving plate and serve hot or at room temperature, cut into wedges.

GOAT CHEESE SOUFFLÉ

Soufflé au Fromage de Chèvre

Make sure everyone is seated before the soufflé comes out of the oven because it will begin to deflate almost immediately. This recipe works equally well with strong blue cheeses such as Roquefort.

SERVES 4–6

2 tbsp butter
3 tbsp flour
¾ cup milk
1 bay leaf
ground nutmeg
grated Parmesan cheese, for
    sprinkling
1½ ounces herb and garlic soft cheese
5 ounces firm goat cheese, diced
6 egg whites, at room temperature
¼ tsp cream of tartar
salt and freshly ground black pepper

1 Melt the butter in a heavy saucepan over medium heat. Add the flour and cook until slightly golden, stirring occasionally. Pour in half the milk, stirring vigorously until smooth, then stir in the remaining milk and add the bay leaf. Season with a pinch of salt and plenty of pepper and nutmeg. Reduce the heat to medium-low, cover and simmer gently for about 5 minutes, stirring occasionally.

2 ▲ Preheat the oven to 375°F. Generously butter a 5 cup soufflé dish and sprinkle with the grated Parmesan cheese.

3 ▼ Remove the sauce from the heat and discard the bay leaf. Stir in both cheeses.

4 In a clean greasefree bowl, using an electric mixer or balloon whisk, beat the egg whites slowly until they become frothy. Add the cream of tartar, increase the speed and continue beating until they form soft peaks, then stiffer peaks that just flop over a little at the top.

5 ▲ Stir a spoonful of beaten egg whites into the cheese sauce to lighten it, then pour the cheese sauce over the remaining whites. Using a rubber spatula or large metal spoon, gently fold the sauce into the whites until the mixtures are just combined, cutting down through the center to the bottom, then along the side of the bowl and up to the top.

6 Gently pour the soufflé mixture into the prepared dish and bake for 25–30 minutes until puffed and golden brown. Serve at once.

VEGETABLES
AND
SIDE
DISHES

The French hold vegetables in high regard,
serving them as a course on their own, or at
least on a separate plate. Even as an
accompaniment, vegetables are usually treated
with the same ingenuity as more expensive
foods – adorned with creative seasonings or
served in unusual combinations. The array of
colorful fresh vegetables in French markets
changes with the seasons and region, but classic
cuisine makes the most of vegetables
in wonderful ways.

RICE PILAF

Riz Pilaf

In France the word pilaf refers to the cooking method of sautéing food in fat before adding liquid. This method produces perfect rice every time.

SERVES 6–8

3 tbsp butter or 3–4 tbsp oil
1 medium onion, finely chopped
2 cups long grain rice
3 cups chicken broth or water
½ tsp dried thyme
1 small bay leaf
salt and freshly ground black pepper
1–2 tbsp chopped fresh parsley, dill or chives, to garnish

COOK'S TIP

Once cooked, the rice will remain hot for half an hour, tightly covered. Or, spoon into a microwave-safe bowl, cover and microwave on High (full power) for about 5 minutes until hot.

---

1 ▼ In a large heavy saucepan, melt the butter or heat the oil over medium heat. Add the onion and cook for 2–3 minutes until just softened, stirring constantly. Add the rice and cook for 1–2 minutes until the rice becomes translucent but does not begin to brown, stirring frequently.

2 ▲ Add the broth or water, dried thyme and bay leaf and season with salt and pepper. Bring to a boil over high heat, stirring frequently. Just as the rice begins to boil, cover the surface with a round of foil or a wax paper circle and cover the saucepan. Reduce the heat to very low and cook for 20 minutes (do not lift the cover or stir). Serve hot, garnished with fresh herbs.

SAUTÉED WILD MUSHROOMS *Champignons Sauvages à la Bordelaise*

This is a quick dish to prepare and makes an ideal accompaniment to all kinds of roast and grilled meats. Use any combination of wild or "cultivated wild" mushrooms you can find.

SERVES 6

2 pounds mixed fresh wild and cultivated mushrooms, such as morels, porcini, chanterelles, oyster or shiitake
2 tbsp olive oil
2 tbsp unsalted butter
2 garlic cloves, finely chopped
3 or 4 shallots, finely chopped
3–4 tbsp chopped fresh parsley, or a mixture of fresh herbs
salt and freshly ground black pepper

1 Wash and carefully dry any very dirty mushrooms. Trim the stems and cut the mushrooms into quarters or slice if very large.

2 ▲ In a large heavy frying pan, heat the oil over medium–high heat. Add the butter and swirl to melt, then stir in the mushrooms and cook for 4–5 minutes until they begin to brown.

3 ▼ Add the garlic and shallots and cook for 4–5 minutes more until the mushrooms are tender and any liquid given off has evaporated. Season with salt and pepper and stir in the parsley or mixed herbs.

CABBAGE CHARLOTTE *Charlotte de Chou et de Pommes de Terre*

This delicious dish takes its name from the steep-sided container with heart-shaped handles in which it is cooked, but any straight-sided dish, such as a soufflé dish, will do.

SERVES 6

1 pound green or savoy cabbage
2 tbsp butter
1 medium onion, chopped
1¼ pounds potatoes, peeled and
*   quartered*
1 large egg, beaten
1–2 tbsp milk, if needed
salt and freshly ground black pepper

1 Preheat the oven to 375°F. Lightly butter a 5 cup charlotte mold or soufflé dish. Line the base with wax paper and butter again. Set the mold aside.

2 Bring a large saucepan of salted water to a boil. Remove 5–6 large leaves from the cabbage and add to the pan. Cook the leaves for about 2 minutes until softened and bright green, then plunge them into cold water. Chop the remaining cabbage.

3 Melt the butter in a heavy frying pan and cook the onion for 2–3 minutes until just softened. Stir in the chopped cabbage and cook, covered, over a medium heat for 10–15 minutes until tender and pale golden, stirring frequently.

4 ▲ Put the potatoes in a large saucepan and add enough cold water to cover. Salt the water generously and bring to a boil over medium-high heat. Cook until the potatoes are tender, then drain. Mash them with the beaten egg and a little milk, if needed, until smooth and creamy, then stir in the cabbage mixture. Season with salt and pepper.

5 ▲ Dry the cabbage leaves and cut out the thickest part of the center vein. Use the leaves to line the mold, saving one leaf for the top. Spoon the potato mixture into the dish, smoothing it evenly, then cover with the remaining cabbage leaf. Cover tightly with foil. Put the mold in a shallow roasting pan or a baking dish and pour in boiling water to come halfway up the side of the mold. Bake for 40 minutes.

6 To serve, remove the foil and place a serving plate over the mold. Holding the plate tightly against the mold, turn over together. Lift off the mold and peel off the paper.

STUFFED ARTICHOKE BOTTOMS *Fonds d'Artichauts aux Duxelles*

This recipe is a partnership of two favorites of classic French cuisine: duxelles – *the savory chopped mushrooms used in the filling – and the artichoke with its distinctive delicate flavor.*

SERVES 4–6

8 ounces button mushrooms
1 tbsp butter
2 shallots, finely chopped
2 ounces full- or medium-fat soft cheese
2 tbsp chopped walnuts
3 tbsp grated Swiss cheese
4 large or 6 small artichoke bottoms
    (from cooked artichokes, leaves and
    choke removed, or cooked frozen or
    canned artichoke bottoms)
salt and freshly ground black pepper
fresh parsley sprigs, to garnish

1 ▲ Wipe or rinse the mushrooms and pat dry. Put them in a food processor fitted with the metal blade and pulse until finely chopped.

2 ▲ Melt the butter in a non-stick frying pan and cook the shallots over medium heat for 2–3 minutes until just softened. Add the mushrooms, raise the heat slightly, and cook for 5–7 minutes until they have rendered and reabsorbed their liquid and are almost dry, stirring frequently. Season with salt and pepper.

3 Preheat the oven to 400°F. Lightly grease a shallow baking pan or dish.

4 ▼ In a small bowl, combine the soft cheese and mushrooms. Add the walnuts and half the grated cheese.

5 ▲ Divide the mushroom mixture among the artichoke bottoms and arrange them in the baking pan or dish. Sprinkle over the remaining cheese and bake for 12–15 minutes, or until bubbly and browned. Serve hot, garnished with parsley sprigs.

PEAS WITH LETTUCE AND ONION   *Petits Pois à la Française*

Fresh peas vary enormously in the time they take to cook – the tastiest and sweetest will be young and just picked. Frozen peas normally need less cooking time than fresh.

SERVES 4–6

1 tbsp butter
1 small onion, finely chopped
1 small round lettuce
3½ cups shelled fresh peas (from about
 3½ pounds peas), or thawed
 frozen peas
3 tbsp water
salt and freshly ground black pepper

1 Melt the butter in a heavy saucepan. Add the onion and cook over medium-low heat for about 3 minutes until just softened.

2 ▼ Cut the lettuce in half through the core, then place cut side down on a board and slice into thin strips. Place the lettuce strips on top of the onion and add the peas and water. Season lightly with salt and pepper.

3 ▲ Cover the pan tightly and cook the lettuce and peas over low heat until the peas are tender – fresh peas will take 10–20 minutes, frozen peas about 10 minutes.

FAVA BEANS WITH CREAM   *Fèves à la Crème*

In France, tiny new fava beans are eaten raw with a little salt, just like radishes. More mature fava beans are usually cooked and skinned, revealing the bright green kernel inside.

SERVES 4–6

1 pound shelled fava beans (from about
 4½ pounds fava beans)
6 tbsp crème fraîche or heavy cream
salt and freshly ground black pepper
finely snipped chives, to garnish

1 ▼ Bring a large pan of salted water to a boil over medium-high heat and add the beans.

2 Bring back to the boil, then reduce the heat slightly and boil the beans gently for about 8 minutes until just tender. Drain and refresh in cold water, then drain again.

3 ▲ To remove the skins, make an opening along one side of each bean with the tip of a knife and gently squeeze out the kernel.

4 ▲ Put the skinned beans in a saucepan with the cream and seasoning, cover and heat through gently. Sprinkle with the snipped chives and serve.

VARIATION

Young, tender fresh lima beans are delicious served in the same way.

SAUTÉED POTATOES

Pommes de Terre Sautées au Romarin

These rosemary-scented, crisp golden potatoes are a favorite in French households.

SERVES 6

3 pounds baking potatoes
4–6 tbsp oil, bacon drippings or
  clarified butter
2 or 3 fresh rosemary sprigs, leaves
  removed and chopped
salt and freshly ground black pepper

1 Peel the potatoes and cut into 1 inch pieces. Place them in a bowl, cover with cold water and let soak for 10–15 minutes. Drain, rinse and drain again, then dry thoroughly in a kitchen towel.

2 In a nonstick large heavy frying pan or wok, heat about 4 tbsp of the oil, drippings or butter over a medium–high heat, until very hot, but not smoking.

3 ▲ Add the potatoes and cook for 2 minutes without stirring so that they seal completely and brown on one side.

4 Shake the pan and toss the potatoes to brown on another side and continue to stir and shake the pan until potatoes are evenly browned on all sides. Season with salt and pepper.

5 ▼ Add a little more oil, drippings or butter and continue cooking the potatoes over medium-low to low heat for 20–25 minutes until tender when pierced with a knife, stirring and shaking the pan frequently. About 5 minutes before the potatoes are done, sprinkle them with the chopped rosemary.

STRAW POTATO CAKE

Pommes Paillasson

These potatoes are so named in France because of their resemblance to a woven straw doormat. You could make several small cakes instead of a large one – just adjust the cooking time accordingly.

SERVES 4

1 pound baking potatoes
1½ tbsp melted butter
1 tbsp vegetable oil, plus more
  if needed
salt and freshly ground black pepper

1 Peel the potatoes and grate them coarsely, then immediately toss them with the melted butter and season with salt and pepper.

2 ▲ Heat the oil in a large frying pan. Add the potato mixture and press down to form an even layer that covers the pan. Cook over medium heat for 7–10 minutes until the base is well browned.

3 Loosen the potato cake by shaking the pan or running a thin spatula under it.

4 ▼ To turn it over, invert a large baking tray over the frying pan and, holding it tightly against the pan, turn them both over together. Lift off the frying pan, return it to the heat and add a little oil if it looks dry. Slide the potato cake into the frying pan and continue cooking until crisp and browned on both sides. Serve hot.

FISH
AND
SHELLFISH

The bounty of the sea brings fresh elegance to your entertaining. Most fish and shellfish are quick and easy to cook and offer limitless versatility. In a celebration dinner, seafood is the classic first course. Served as a main course, even when prepared with a rich sauce, it is light enough to follow a substantial first course or precede a voluptuous dessert. Ease of preparation makes fish and shellfish the perfect choice for bringing a bit of French festivity to family suppers as well.

SOLE WITH SHRIMP AND MUSSELS   *Filets de Sole à la Dieppoise*

This classic regional specialty takes its name from the Normandy port of Dieppe, renowned for fish and seafood. The recipe incorporates another great product of the region – cream.

SERVES 6

6 tbsp butter
8 shallots, finely chopped
1¼ cups dry white wine
2¼ pounds mussels, scrubbed and debearded
8 ounces button mushrooms, quartered
1 cup fish stock
12 skinless lemon or Dover sole fillets (about 3–5 ounces each)
2 tbsp flour
4 tbsp crème fraîche or heavy cream
8 ounces cooked, peeled shrimp
salt and white pepper
fresh parsley sprigs, to garnish

2 ▲ Transfer the mussels to a large bowl. Strain the mussel cooking liquid through a cheesecloth-lined colander and set aside. When cool enough to handle, reserve a few mussels in their shells for the garnish. Then remove the rest from their shells and set aside, covered.

4 ▲ Melt the remaining butter in a small saucepan over medium heat. Add the flour and cook for 1–2 minutes, stirring constantly; do not allow the flour mixture to brown. Gradually whisk in the reduced fish cooking liquid, the reserved mussel liquid and pour in any liquid from the fish, then bring to a boil, stirring constantly.

1 ▲ In a large heavy flameproof casserole, melt 1 tbsp of the butter over medium-high heat. Add half the shallots and cook for about 2 minutes until just softened, stirring frequently. Add the white wine and bring to a boil, then add the mussels and cover tightly. Cook the mussels over high heat, shaking and tossing the pan occasionally, for 4–5 minutes until the shells open. Discard any mussels that do not open.

3 ▲ Melt half the remaining butter in a large heavy frying pan over medium heat. Add the remaining shallots and cook for 2 minutes until just softened, stirring frequently. Add the mushrooms and fish stock and bring just to the simmer. Season the fish fillets with salt and pepper. Fold or roll them and slide gently into the stock. Cover and poach for 5–7 minutes until the flesh is opaque. Transfer the fillets to a warmed serving dish and cover to keep warm. Increase the heat and boil the liquid until reduced by one-third.

5 ▲ Reduce the heat to medium-low and cook the sauce for 5–7 minutes, stirring frequently. Whisk in the crème fraîche or heavy cream and keep stirring over low heat until well blended. Adjust the seasoning then add the reserved mussels and the shrimp to the sauce. Cook gently for 2–3 minutes to heat through then spoon the sauce over the fish and serve garnished with fresh parsley sprigs.

GRILLED RED SNAPPER WITH HERBS   *Rouget Grillé aux Herbes*

In Provence this fish is often charcoal-grilled with herbs from the region or dried fennel branches.

SERVES 4

olive oil, for brushing
4 red snapper (8–10 ounces each),
    cleaned and scaled
fresh herb sprigs, such as parsley, dill,
    basil or thyme
dried fennel branches
2–3 tbsp Pernod (or other anise-flavored
    liqueur)

1 About one hour before cooking, light a charcoal fire: when ready the coals should be gray with no flames. Generously brush a hinged grilling rack with olive oil.

2 ▲ Brush each fish with a little olive oil and stuff the cavity with a few herb sprigs, breaking them to fit if necessary. Secure the fish in the grilling rack. Lay the dried fennel branches over the coals and grill the fish for about 15–20 minutes, turning once during cooking.

3 ▼ Remove the fish to a warmed, flameproof serving dish. Pour the liqueur into a small saucepan and heat for a moment or two, then tilt the pan and carefully ignite with a long match. Pour evenly over the fish and serve at once.

SALMON STEAKS WITH SORREL SAUCE   *Saumon à l'Oseille*

Salmon and sorrel are traditionally paired in France – the sharp flavor of the sorrel balances the richness of the fish. If sorrel is not available, use finely chopped watercress instead.

SERVES 2

2 salmon steaks (about 8 ounces each)
1 tsp olive oil
1 tbsp butter
2 shallots, finely chopped
3 tbsp heavy cream
3½ ounces fresh sorrel leaves, washed
    and patted dry
salt and freshly ground black pepper
fresh sage, to garnish

COOK'S TIP

If preferred, cook the salmon steaks in a microwave oven for about 4–5 minutes, tightly covered, or according to the manufacturer's guidelines.

---

1 Season the salmon steaks with salt and pepper. Brush a non-stick frying pan with the oil.

2 ▲ In a small saucepan, melt the butter over medium heat and fry the shallots, stirring frequently, until just softened. Add the cream and the sorrel to the shallots and cook until the sorrel is completely wilted, stirring constantly.

3 ▲ Meanwhile, heat the frying pan over medium heat until hot. Add the salmon steaks and cook for about 5 minutes, turning once, until the flesh is opaque next to the bone. If you're not sure, pierce with the tip of a sharp knife; the juices should run clear. Arrange the salmon steaks on two warmed plates, garnish with sage and serve with the sorrel sauce.

TROUT WITH ALMONDS   *Truites aux Amandes*

This simple and quick recipe doubles easily – you can cook the trout in two frying pans or in batches. In Normandy, hazelnuts might be used in place of almonds.

SERVES 2

2 trout (about 12 ounces each), cleaned
⅓ cup flour
4 tbsp butter
¼ cup slivered or sliced almonds
2 tbsp dry white wine
salt and freshly ground black pepper

1 Rinse the trout and pat dry. Put the flour in a large plastic bag and season with salt and pepper. Place the trout, one at a time, in the bag and shake to coat with flour. Shake off the excess flour from the fish and discard the remaining flour.

2 ▲ Melt half the butter in a large frying pan over medium heat. When it is foamy, add the trout and cook for 6–7 minutes on each side, until golden brown and the flesh next to the bone is opaque. Transfer the fish to warmed plates and cover to keep warm.

3 ▼ Add the remaining butter to the pan and cook the almonds until just lightly browned. Add the wine to the pan and boil for 1 minute, stirring constantly, until slightly syrupy. Pour or spoon over the fish and serve at once.

TUNA WITH GARLIC, TOMATOES AND HERBS   *Thon St Rémy*

St Rémy is a beautiful village in Provence in the South of France. Herbs, such as thyme, rosemary and oregano, grow wild on the nearby hillsides and feature in many of the recipes from this area.

SERVES 4

4 tuna steaks, about 1 inch thick
    (6–7 ounces each)
2–3 tbsp olive oil
3 or 4 garlic cloves, finely chopped
4 tbsp dry white wine
3 ripe plum tomatoes, peeled, seeded
    and chopped
1 tsp dried herbes de Provence
salt and freshly ground black pepper
fresh basil leaves, to garnish

COOK'S TIP

Tuna is often served pink in the middle like beef. If you prefer it cooked through, reduce the heat and cook for an extra few minutes.

1 ▼ Season the tuna steaks with salt and pepper. Heat a heavy frying pan over high heat until very hot, add the oil and swirl to coat. Add the tuna steaks and press down gently, then reduce the heat to medium and cook for 6–8 minutes, turning once, until just slightly pink in the center.

2 ▲ Transfer the steaks to a serving plate and cover to keep warm. Add the garlic to the pan and fry for 15–20 seconds, stirring constantly, then pour in the wine and boil until it is reduced by half. Add the tomatoes and dried herbs and cook for 2–3 minutes until the sauce is bubbly. Season with pepper and pour over the fish steaks. Serve, garnished with fresh basil leaves.

SHELLFISH WITH SEASONED BROTH

Fruits de Mer à la Nage

Leave one or two mussels and shrimp in their shells to add a flamboyant touch to this elegant dish.

SERVES 4

1½ pounds mussels, scrubbed and
    debearded
1 small fennel bulb, thinly sliced
1 onion, finely sliced
1 leek, thinly sliced
1 small carrot, cut in julienne strips
1 garlic clove
4 cups water
pinch of curry powder
pinch of saffron
1 bay leaf
1 pound large shrimp, peeled
1 pound scallops
6 ounces cooked lobster meat, sliced
    (optional)
1–2 tbsp chopped fresh chervil
    or parsley
salt and freshly ground black pepper

1 ▼ Put the mussels in a large heavy saucepan or flameproof casserole and cook, tightly covered, over high heat for 4–6 minutes until the shells open, shaking the pan or casserole occasionally. When cool enough to handle, discard any mussels that did not open and remove the rest from their shells. Strain the cooking liquid through a cheesecloth-lined strainer and reserve.

2 ▲ Put the fennel, onion, leek, carrot and garlic in a saucepan and add the water, reserved mussel liquid, spices and bay leaf. Bring to a boil, skimming any foam that rises to the surface, then reduce the heat and simmer gently, covered, for 20 minutes until the vegetables are tender. Remove the garlic clove.

3 ▲ Add the shrimp, scallops and lobster meat, if using, then after 1 minute, add the mussels. Simmer gently for about 3 minutes until the scallops are opaque and all the shellfish is heated through. Adjust the seasoning, then ladle into a heated tureen or shallow soup plates and sprinkle with herbs.

COOK'S TIP

If you like, you can cook and shell the mussels and simmer the vegetables in the broth ahead of time, then finish the dish just before serving.

LOBSTER THERMIDOR

Homard Thermidor

Lobster Thermidor takes its name from the 11th month of the French Revolutionary calendar, which falls in midsummer, although this rich dish is equally delicious in cooler weather, too. Serve one lobster per person as a main course or one filled shell each for a first course.

SERVES 2–4

2 live lobsters (about 1½ pounds each)
1½ tbsp butter
2 tbsp flour
30ml/2 tbsp brandy
125ml/4fl oz/½ cup milk
90ml/6 tbsp whipping cream
1 tbsp Dijon mustard
lemon juice
salt and white pepper
grated Parmesan cheese, for sprinkling
fresh parsley and dill, to garnish

3 ▲ Melt the butter in a heavy saucepan over medium-high heat. Stir in the flour and cook, stirring, until slightly golden. Pour in the brandy and milk, whisking vigorously until smooth, then whisk in the cream and mustard.

4 Push the lobster coral and liver through a sieve into the sauce and whisk to blend. Reduce the heat to low and simmer gently for about 10 minutes, stirring frequently, until thickened. Season with salt, if needed, pepper and lemon juice.

5 Preheat the broiler. Arrange the lobster shells in a gratin dish or shallow flameproof baking dish.

6 Stir the lobster meat into the sauce and divide the mixture evenly among the shells. Sprinkle lightly with Parmesan and grill until golden. Serve garnished with herbs.

1 ▲ Bring a large saucepan of salted water to a boil. Put the lobsters into the pan head first and cook for 8–10 minutes.

2 ▲ Cut the lobsters in half lengthwise and discard the dark sac behind the eyes, then pull out the string-like intestine from the tail. Remove the meat from the shells, reserving the coral and liver, then rinse the shells and wipe dry. Cut the meat into bite-size pieces.

MEAT DISHES

Meat makes a memorable main course, whether it's a classic roast, a quick sauté or a rich stew. All of these meat dishes bring an elegant French touch to your special occasions and each have their advantages. Stews can be mostly prepared in advance, leaving only finishing touches to be done before serving. A roast needs little attention and lets the cook work on other things. A few of these recipes need a bit more last-minute preparation, but you will find the results are worthwhile.

WHITE VEAL STEW

Blanquette de Veau

A blanquette is a "white" stew traditionally enriched with cream and egg yolks. This bistro favorite is usually made with veal, but in the South of France, it is often made with lamb.

SERVES 6

*3 pounds boneless veal shoulder, cut into
    2 inch pieces
6¼ cups veal or chicken broth or water
    (or more if needed)
1 large onion, studded with 2 cloves
4 carrots, sliced
2 leeks, sliced
1 garlic clove, halved
bouquet garni
1 tbsp black peppercorns
5 tbsp butter
½lb button mushrooms, quartered if
    large
½lb pearl onions
1 tbsp superfine sugar
¼ cup flour
½ cup crème fraîche or heavy cream
pinch of ground nutmeg
2–4 tbsp chopped fresh dill
    or parsley
salt and white pepper*

1 Put the veal in a large flameproof casserole and cover with the broth or water. Bring to a boil over medium heat, skimming off any foam that rises to the surface.

2 ▲ Add the studded onion, one of the sliced carrots, the leeks, garlic, bouquet garni and peppercorns, then cover and simmer over medium-low heat for about 1 hour until the veal is just tender.

3 ▲ Meanwhile, in a frying pan, melt 1 tbsp of the butter over medium-high heat, add the mushrooms and sauté until lightly golden. Transfer to a large bowl using a slotted spoon.

4 ▲ Add another 1 tbsp butter to the pan and add the pearl onions. Sprinkle with the sugar and add about 6 tbsp of the veal cooking liquid, then cover and simmer for 10–12 minutes until the onions are tender and the liquid has evaporated. Transfer the onions to the bowl with the mushrooms.

COOK'S TIP

If you would like to use the traditional egg and cream mixture, stir the cream into two beaten egg yolks before whisking into the white sauce and proceed as above. Simmer until the sauce thickens, but do not allow the sauce to boil or it may curdle.

5 ▲ When the veal is tender, transfer it to the same bowl using a slotted spoon. Strain the cooking liquid and discard the cooked vegetables and bouquet garni, then wash the casserole and return it to the heat.

6 ▲ Melt the remaining butter, add the flour and cook for 1–2 minutes over medium heat, but do not allow the mixture to brown. Slowly whisk in the reserved cooking liquid and bring to a boil, then simmer the sauce for 15–20 minutes until smooth and slightly thickened. Add the remaining carrots and cook for 10 minutes more until tender.

7 Whisk the cream into the sauce and simmer until the sauce is slightly thickened. Return the reserved meat, mushrooms and onions to the sauce and simmer for 10–15 minutes until the veal is very tender, skimming and stirring occasionally. Season with salt and white pepper and a little nutmeg, then stir in the chopped dill or parsley and serve.

FILET MIGNON WITH MUSHROOMS $\qquad$ *Tournedos Rossini*

In the time of Escoffier, this haute cuisine dish was made with truffle slices but large mushroom caps are more readily available and look attractive, especially when they are fluted.

SERVES 4

4 thin slices white bread
*4 ounces pâté de foie gras or mousse
    de foie gras*
5 tbsp butter
4 large mushroom caps
2 tsp vegetable oil
4 fillet steaks (about 1 inch thick)
3–4 tbsp Madeira or port
½ cup beef broth
watercress, to garnish

COOK'S TIP

If *pâté de foie gras* is difficult to
find, you could substitute
pork liver pâté.

1 ▼ Cut the bread into rounds about the same diameter as the steaks, using a large round cutter or by cutting into squares, then cutting off the corners. Toast the bread and spread with the *foie gras*, dividing it evenly. Place the croûtons on warmed plates.

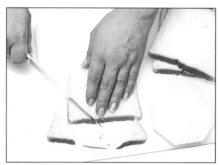

2 ▲ Flute the mushroom caps using the edge of a knife blade, if you wish, for a decorative effect. Melt about 2 tbsp of the butter over medium heat and sauté the mushrooms until golden. Transfer to a plate and keep warm.

3 ▲ In the same pan, melt another 2 tbsp of the butter with the oil over medium-high heat, swirling to combine. When the butter begins to brown, add the steaks and cook for 6–8 minutes, turning once, until done as preferred (medium-rare meat will still be slightly soft when pressed, medium will be springy and well-done firm). Place the steaks on the croûtons and top with the mushroom caps.

4 Add the Madeira or port to the pan and boil for 20–30 seconds. Add the broth and boil over high heat until reduced by three-quarters, then swirl in the remaining butter. Pour a little sauce over each steak, then garnish with watercress.

PEPPER STEAK   *Steak au Poivre*

There are many versions of this French bistro classic; some omit the cream, but it helps to balance the heat of the pepper. Use fairly thick steaks, such as fillet or lean sirloin.

SERVES 2

2 tbsp black peppercorns
2 fillet or sirloin steaks, about
8 ounces each
1 tbsp butter
2 tsp vegetable oil
3 tbsp brandy
⅔ cup heavy cream
1 garlic clove, finely chopped
salt, if needed

1 ▲ Place the peppercorns in a sturdy plastic bag. Crush with a rolling pin until medium-coarse or, using the flat base of a small heavy saucepan, press down on the peppercorns, rocking the pan to crush them.

2 ▲ Put the steaks on a board and trim away any extra fat. Press the pepper onto both sides of the meat, coating it completely.

3 ▼ Melt the butter with the oil in a heavy frying pan over medium-high heat. Add the meat and cook for 6–7 minutes, turning once, until done as preferred (medium-rare meat will still be slightly soft when pressed, medium will be springy and well-done firm). Transfer the steaks to a warmed platter or plates and cover to keep warm.

4 ▲ Pour in the brandy to deglaze the pan. Allow to boil until reduced by half, scraping the base of the pan, then add the cream and garlic. Boil gently over medium heat for about 4 minutes until the cream has reduced by one-third. Stir any accumulated juices from the meat into the sauce, taste and add salt, if necessary, then serve the steaks with the sauce.

ROAST STUFFED LAMB   *Gigot Farci*

The lambs that graze in the salty marshes along the north coast of Brittany and Normandy are considered the best in France. The stuffing is suitable for either leg or shoulder joints.

SERVES 6–8

*4–4½ pound boneless leg or shoulder of
    lamb (not tied)
2 tbsp butter, softened
1–2 tbsp flour
½ cup white wine
1 cup chicken or beef broth
salt and freshly ground black pepper
watercress, to garnish
sautéed potatoes, to serve*
FOR THE STUFFING
*5 tbsp butter
1 small onion, finely chopped
1 garlic clove, finely chopped
⅓ cup long grain rice
⅔ cup chicken broth
½ tsp dried thyme
4 lamb kidneys, halved and cored
10 ounces young spinach leaves,
    well washed
salt and freshly ground black pepper*

1 ▲ To make the stuffing, melt 2 tbsp of the butter in a saucepan over medium heat. Add the onion and cook for 2–3 minutes until just softened, then add the garlic and rice and cook for about 1–2 minutes until the rice appears translucent, stirring constantly. Add the broth, salt and pepper and thyme and bring to a boil, stirring occasionally, then reduce the heat to low and cook for about 18 minutes, covered, until the rice is tender and the liquid is absorbed. Spoon the rice into a bowl and fluff with a fork.

2 In a small frying pan, melt about 2 tbsp of the remaining butter over medium-high heat. Add the kidneys and cook for about 2–3 minutes, turning once, until lightly browned, but still pink inside, then transfer to a board and let cool. Cut the kidneys into pieces and add to the rice, season with salt and pepper and toss to combine.

3 ▲ In a frying pan, heat the remaining butter over medium heat until foaming. Add the spinach leaves and cook for 1–2 minutes until wilted, drain off excess liquid, then transfer the spinach to a plate and let cool.

4 ▲ Preheat the oven to 375°F. Lay the meat skin-side down on a work surface and season with salt and pepper. Spread the spinach leaves in an even layer over the surface then spread the stuffing in an even layer over the spinach. Roll up the meat like a jelly roll and use a skewer to close the seam.

5 ▲ Tie the meat at 1 inch intervals to hold its shape, then place in a roasting pan, spread with the softened butter and season with salt and pepper. Roast for 1½–2 hours until the juices run slightly pink when pierced with a skewer, or until a meat thermometer inserted into the thickest part of the meat registers 135–140°F for medium-rare to medium. Transfer the meat to a carving board, cover loosely with foil and let rest for about 20 minutes.

6 Skim off as much fat from the roasting pan as possible, then place the pan over medium-high heat and bring to a boil. Sprinkle over the flour and cook for 2–3 minutes until browned, stirring and scraping the base of the pan. Whisk in the wine and broth and bring to a boil, then cook for 4–5 minutes until the sauce thickens. Season and strain into a gravy boat. Carve the meat into slices, garnish with watercress and serve with the gravy and potatoes.

VARIATION

If kidneys are difficult to obtain, substitute about ¼ pound mushrooms. Chop coarsely and cook in butter until tender. Don't use dark mushrooms – they will make the rice a murky color.

PORK WITH CAMEMBERT   *Médaillons de Porc au Camembert*

Not surprisingly, most cheese-producing regions of France have a tradition of recipes using their own home-produced cheese. This recipe combines several of the fine products of Normandy.

SERVES 3–4

¾–1 pound pork tenderloin
1 tbsp butter
3 tbsp sparkling dry cider or dry white
    wine
½–¾ cup crème fraîche or heavy cream
1 tbsp chopped fresh mixed herbs, such as
    marjoram, thyme and sage
½ Camembert cheese (4 ounces), rind
    removed (2½ ounces without
    rind), sliced
1½ tsp Dijon mustard
freshly ground black pepper
fresh parsley, to garnish

1 ▼ Slice the pork tenderloin crosswise into small steaks about ¾ inch thick. Place between two sheets of wax paper or plastic wrap and pound with the flat side of a meat mallet or roll with a rolling pin to flatten to a thickness of ½ inch. Sprinkle with pepper.

2 ▲ Melt the butter in a heavy frying pan over medium-high heat until it begins to brown, then add the meat. Cook for 5 minutes, turning once, or until just cooked through and the meat is springy when pressed. Transfer to a warmed dish and cover to keep warm.

3 ▲ Add the cider or wine and bring to a boil, scraping the base of the pan. Stir in the cream and herbs and bring back to a boil.

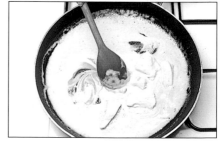

4 ▲ Add the cheese and mustard and any accumulated juices from the meat. Add a little more cream if needed and adjust the seasoning. Serve the pork with the sauce and garnish with parsley.

BRAISED HAM WITH MADIERA SAUCE   *Jambon Braisé au Madère*

The Morvan district of Burgundy is known for producing fine quality, mild cured hams. Accompanied by this rich Madeira sauce, a simple ham steak is transformed into an elegant dish.

SERVES 4

4 tbsp unsalted butter
4 shallots, finely chopped
2 tbsp flour
2 cups beef broth
1 tbsp tomato paste
6 tbsp Madeira
4 ham steaks (about 6–7 ounces
    each)
salt and freshly ground black pepper
watercress, to garnish
mashed potatoes, to serve

1 ▲ Melt half the butter in a heavy medium-size saucepan, over medium-high heat, then add the shallots and cook for 2–3 minutes until just softened, stirring frequently.

2 ▲ Sprinkle over the flour and cook for 3–4 minutes until well browned, stirring constantly, then whisk in the stock and tomato paste and season with pepper. Simmer over low heat until the sauce is reduced by about half, stirring occasionally.

3 ▼ Taste the sauce and adjust the seasoning, then stir in the Madeira and cook for 2–3 minutes. Strain into a small serving bowl or gravy boat and keep warm. (The sauce can be made up to three days in advance and chilled. Reheat to serve.)

COOK'S TIP

To make the sauce a deeper, richer color, add a few drops of gravy browning liquid to the stock.

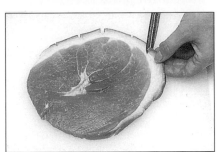

4 ▲ Snip the edges of the ham steaks to prevent them from curling. Melt the remaining butter in a large heavy frying pan over medium-high heat, then add the ham steaks and cook for 4–5 minutes, turning once, until the meat feels firm to the touch. Arrange the ham steaks on warmed plates and pour a little sauce over each. Garnish with watercress and serve the steaks with a little more of the sauce accompanied by mashed potatoes.

POULTRY
AND
GAME

If you want something a little different as a
main course, think of poultry or game. The
French have a rich heritage of poultry dishes
and are particularly fond of game. The
selections in this chapter will bring real French
flair to your table, and strategies for advance
preparation make them easy to cook.
Traditional yet novel combinations like chicken
with grapes and classics such as the recipes for
duck and venison will make your special
occasions really memorable.

QUAIL WITH FRESH FIGS

Cailles aux Figues Fraîches

The fig trees in the South of France are laden with ripe purple fruit in early autumn, coinciding with the quail shooting season.

SERVES 4

8 oven-ready quail (5 ounces each)
6 firm ripe figs, quartered
1 tbsp butter
6 tbsp dry sherry
1¼ cups chicken broth
1 garlic clove, finely chopped
2–3 thyme sprigs
1 bay leaf
1½ tsp cornstarch blended with 1 tbsp
  water
salt and freshly ground black pepper
green salad, to serve

1 ▼ Season the quail inside and out with salt and pepper. Put a fig quarter in the cavity of each quail and tie the legs with string.

2 ▲ Melt the butter in a deep frying pan or heavy flameproof casserole over medium-high heat. Add the quail and cook for 5–6 minutes, turning to brown all sides evenly; cook in batches if necessary.

3 ▲ Add the sherry and boil for 1 minute, then add the broth, garlic, thyme and bay leaf. Bring slowly to a boil, reduce the heat and simmer gently, covered, for about 20 minutes.

4 Add the remaining fig quarters and continue cooking for 5 minutes more until the juices run clear when the thigh of a quail is pierced with a knife. Transfer the quail and figs to a warmed serving dish, cut off the trussing string and cover to keep warm.

5 Bring the sauce to a boil, then stir in the blended cornstarch. Cook gently for 3 minutes, stirring frequently, until the sauce is thickened, then strain into a sauceboat. Serve the quail and figs with the sauce and a green salad.

CHICKEN CHASSEUR

Poulet Sauté Chasseur

A chicken sauté is one of the classics of French cooking. Quick to prepare, it lends itself to endless variation. Since this dish reheats successfully, it is also convenient for entertaining.

SERVES 4

¼ cup flour
2½ pounds chicken pieces
1 tbsp olive oil
3 small onions or large shallots, sliced
6 ounces mushrooms, quartered
1 garlic clove, crushed
4 tbsp dry white wine
½ cup chicken broth
¾ pound tomatoes, peeled, seeded and
    chopped, or 1 cup canned crushed
    tomatoes
salt and freshly ground black pepper
fresh parsley, to garnish

3 ▲ Pour off all but 1 tbsp of fat from the pan. Add the onions or shallots, mushrooms and garlic. Cook until golden, stirring frequently.

COOK'S TIP

To prepare ahead, reduce the cooking time by 5 minutes. Let cool and chill. Reheat gently for 15–20 minutes.

4 ▼ Return the chicken to the casserole with any juices. Add the wine and bring to a boil, then stir in the broth and tomatoes. Bring back to a boil, reduce the heat, cover and simmer over low heat for about 20 minutes until the chicken is tender and the juices run clear when the thickest part of the meat is pierced with a knife. Tilt the pan and skim off any fat that has risen to the surface, then adjust the seasoning before serving.

1 ▲ Put the flour into a plastic bag and season with salt and pepper. One at a time, drop the chicken pieces into the bag and shake to coat with flour. Carefully tap off the excess flour.

2 ▲ Heat the oil in a heavy flameproof casserole. Fry the chicken over medium-high heat until golden brown, turning once. Transfer to a plate and keep warm.

TARRAGON CHICKEN BREASTS *Suprêmes de Poulet à l'Estragon*

The classic French version of this dish uses a whole chicken, but boneless breasts are quick to cook and elegant. The combination of dried and fresh tarragon makes a wonderfully aromatic sauce.

SERVES 4

4 skinless boneless chicken breasts (about 5–6 ounces each)
½ cup dry white wine
about 1¼ cups chicken broth
1 tbsp dried tarragon
1 garlic clove, finely chopped
¾ cup heavy cream
1 tbsp chopped fresh tarragon
salt and freshly ground black pepper
fresh tarragon sprigs, to garnish

COOK'S TIP

Tarragon is traditionally paired with chicken, but you could of course use chopped fresh basil or parsley instead.

---

1 ▼ Season the chicken breasts lightly with salt and pepper and put them in a saucepan just large enough to hold them in one layer. Pour over the wine and broth, adding more broth to cover, if necessary, then add the dried tarragon and the garlic. Bring just to a simmer over medium heat and cook gently for 8–10 minutes until the juices run clear when the chicken is pierced with a knife.

2 ▲ With a slotted spoon, transfer the chicken to a plate and cover to keep warm. Strain the cooking liquid into a small saucepan, skim off any fat and boil to reduce by two-thirds.

3 Add the cream and boil to reduce by half. Stir in the fresh tarragon and adjust the seasoning. Slice the chicken breasts, spoon over a little sauce and garnish with tarragon.

CHICKEN BREASTS WITH GRAPES *Suprêmes de Volaille Veronique*

When grapes are used in a dish, it is often called "Veronique" or sometimes "à la vigneronne" after the wife of the grape grower. Here they are cooked with chicken in a creamy sauce.

SERVES 4

4 boneless chicken breasts (about 7 ounces each), well trimmed
2 tbsp butter
1 large or 2 small shallots, chopped
½ cup dry white wine
1 cup chicken broth
½ cup heavy cream
1 cup (about 30) seedless green grapes
salt and freshly ground black pepper
fresh parsley, to garnish

1 Season the chicken breasts with salt and pepper. Melt half the butter in a frying pan over medium-high heat and cook the chicken breasts until cooked through and golden.

2 ▲ Transfer the chicken breasts to a plate and cover to keep warm. Add the remaining butter and sauté the shallots until just softened, stirring frequently. Add the wine, bring to a boil and boil to reduce by half, then add the broth and continue boiling to reduce by half again.

3 ▼ Add the cream to the sauce, bring back to a boil, and add any juices from the chicken. Add the grapes and cook gently for 5 minutes. Slice the chicken breasts and serve with the sauce, garnished with parsley.

VENISON WITH ROQUEFORT BUTTER   *Chevreuil au Roquefort*

If venison is difficult to find, use beef instead.

SERVES 2

2 venison sirloin steaks, about
*   5–6 ounces each*
1 garlic clove, finely chopped
4 tbsp brandy
3 tbsp unsalted butter
1½ ounces Roquefort cheese
freshly ground black pepper

1 ▲ Put the steaks in a small glass dish. Sprinkle with pepper and garlic and pour over the brandy.

2 Cover the dish and marinate in a cool place, for up to 1 hour, or chill for up to 4 hours.

3 ▲ Using a fork, mash together 2 tbsp of the butter and the cheese, or blend them in a food processor. Shape the mixture into a log, wrap and chill until needed.

4 Heat the remaining butter in a heavy frying pan over medium-high heat. Drain the meat, reserving the marinade.

5 ▲ Add the steaks to the pan. Cook for about 5 minutes, turning once, until the meat is springy to the touch for medium-rare or firmer for more well done, then transfer the steaks to warmed plates.

6 Add the reserved marinade to the pan and bring to a boil, scraping the base of the pan. Pour over the meat, then top each steak with one or two slices of the Roquefort butter and serve.

DUCK WITH PEPPERCORNS   *Magret de Canard au Poivre*

Thick meaty duck breast, like steak, should be served medium-rare. Green peppercorn sauce is popular in modern French bistros, but you can also use somewhat milder pink peppercorns.

SERVES 2

1 tsp vegetable oil
2 duck breasts (about 8 ounces each),
*   skinned*
4 tbsp chicken or duck stock
6 tbsp whipping cream
1 tsp Dijon mustard
1 tbsp pink or green peppercorns in
*   vinegar, drained*
salt
fresh parsley, to garnish

1 Heat the oil in a heavy frying pan. Add the duck breasts and cook over a medium-high heat for about 3 minutes on each side.

2 ▲ Transfer the duck breasts to a plate and cover to keep warm. Pour off any fat from the pan and stir in the stock, cream, mustard and peppercorns. Boil for 2–3 minutes until the sauce thickens slightly, then season with salt.

3 ▼ Pour any accumulated juices from the duck into the sauce, then slice the breasts diagonally. Arrange them on two warmed serving plates, pour over a little of the sauce and garnish with parsley.

ROAST PHEASANT WITH PORT *Faisan Rôti au Porto*

Roasting the pheasant in foil keeps the flesh particularly moist. This recipe is best for very young birds and, if you have a choice, request the more tender female birds.

SERVES 4

*2 oven-ready hen pheasants (about
    1½ pounds each)*
4 tbsp unsalted butter, softened
8 fresh thyme sprigs
2 bay leaves
6 bacon slices
1 tbsp flour
*¾ cup game or chicken broth, plus more
    if needed*
1 tbsp red currant jelly
3–4 tbsp port
freshly ground black pepper

1 Preheat the oven to 450°F. Line a large roasting pan with a sheet of strong foil large enough to enclose the pheasants. Lightly brush the foil with oil.

2 ▼ Wipe the pheasants with damp paper towels and remove any extra fat or skin. Using your fingertips, carefully loosen the skin of the breasts. With a round-bladed knife or small spatula, spread the butter between the skin and breast meat of each bird. Tie the legs securely with string then lay the thyme sprigs and a bay leaf over the breast of each bird.

3 ▲ Lay bacon slices over the breasts, place the birds in the foil-lined pan and season with pepper. Bring together the long ends of the foil, fold over securely to enclose, then seal the ends.

4 Roast the birds for 20 minutes, then reduce the oven temperature to 375°F and cook for 40 minutes more. Uncover the birds and roast 10–15 minutes more or until they are browned and the juices run clear when the thigh of a bird is pierced with a knife. Transfer the birds to a board and let stand, covered with clean foil, for 10 minutes before carving.

5 ▲ Pour the juices from the foil into the roasting pan and skim off any fat. Sprinkle in the flour and cook over medium heat, stirring until smooth. Whisk in the broth and red currant jelly and bring to a boil. Simmer until the sauce thickens slightly, adding more broth if needed, then stir in the port and adjust the seasoning. Strain and serve with the pheasant.

BROILED SQUAB CHICKEN

Poussins Grillés

This recipe is suitable for many kinds of small birds, including squab chickens, Cornish game hens and partridges. It would also work with quail, but decrease the cooking time and spread the citrus mixture over, rather than under, the fragile skin.

SERVES 4

2 squab chickens (about 1½ pounds each)
4 tbsp butter, softened
2 tbsp olive oil
2 garlic cloves, crushed
½ tsp dried thyme
¼ tsp cayenne pepper, or to taste
grated rind and juice of 1 unwaxed lemon
grated rind and juice of 1 unwaxed lime
2 tbsp honey
salt and freshly ground black pepper
tomato salad, to serve
fresh dill, to garnish

1 ▲ Using kitchen scissors, cut along both sides of the backbone of each bird; remove and discard. Cut the birds in half along the the breast bone, then using a rolling pin, press down to flatten.

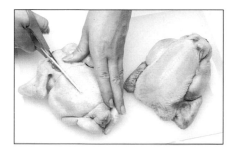

2 ▲ Beat the butter in a small bowl, then beat in 1 tbsp of the olive oil, the garlic, thyme, cayenne, salt and pepper, half the lemon and lime rind and 1 tbsp each of the lemon and lime juice.

3 ▼ Using your fingertips, carefully loosen the skin of each squab chicken breast. With a round-bladed knife or small spatula, spread the butter mixture evenly between the skin and breast meat.

COOK'S TIP

If smaller birds, about 1 pound each, are available, serve one per person. Increase the butter to 6 tbsp, if necessary.

4 ▲ Preheat the broiler and line a broiler pan with foil. In a small bowl, mix together the remaining olive oil, lemon and lime juices and the honey. Place the bird halves, skin side up, on the broiler pan and brush with the juice mixture.

5 Broil for 10–12 minutes, basting once or twice with the juices. Turn over and broil for 7–10 minutes, basting once, or until juices run clear when the thigh is pierced with a knife. Serve with the tomato salad, garnished with dill.

DESSERTS

It is said that first and last courses make the most impact in a meal and dessert, being often the most dramatic course, plays a key role in successful entertaining. This chapter shows that exciting French desserts don't have to be complicated – most of them can be prepared ahead, with minimal, if any, last-minute attention. Classics of French cuisine, such as meringues with chestnut cream and upside-down apple tart, provide lingering memories in the minds of your guests.

POACHED PEACHES WITH RASPBERRY SAUCE *Pêche Melba*

The story goes that one of the great French chefs, Auguste Escoffier, created this dessert in honor of the opera singer Nellie Melba, now forever enshrined in culinary, if not musical, history.

SERVES 6

4 cups water
¼ cup superfine sugar
1 vanilla bean, split lengthwise
3 large peaches
FOR THE RASPBERRY SAUCE
1 pound fresh or frozen raspberries
1 tbsp lemon juice
2–3 tbsp superfine sugar
2–3 tbsp raspberry liqueur (optional)
vanilla ice cream, to serve
mint leaves, to decorate

1 In a saucepan large enough to hold the peach halves in a single layer, combine the water, sugar and vanilla bean. Bring to a boil over medium heat, stirring occasionally to dissolve the sugar.

2 ▼ Cut the peaches in half and twist the halves to separate them. Using a small teaspoon, remove the peach pits. Add the peach halves to the poaching syrup, cut-sides down, adding more water, if needed to cover the fruit. Press a piece of wax paper against the surface of the poaching syrup, reduce the heat to medium-low, then cover and simmer for 12–15 minutes until tender – the time will depend on the ripeness of the fruit. Remove the pan from the heat and let the peaches cool in the syrup.

3 ▲ Remove the peaches from the syrup and peel off the skins. Place on several thicknesses of paper towels to drain (reserve the syrup for another use), then cover and chill.

4 ▲ Put the raspberries, lemon juice and sugar in a food processor fitted with the metal blade. Process for 1 minute, scraping down the sides once. Press through a fine strainer into a small bowl, then stir in the raspberry liqueur, if using, and chill.

5 To serve, place a peach half, cut-side up on a dessert plate, fill with a scoop of vanilla ice cream and spoon the raspberry sauce over the ice cream. Decorate with mint leaves.

COOK'S TIP

Prepare the peaches and sauce up to one day in advance. Leave the peaches in the syrup and cover them and the sauce before chilling.

ICED COFFEE AND NUT MERINGUE *Dacquoise Givrée*

This impressive frozen dessert may seem difficult, but it is actually very easy to prepare.

SERVES 8–10

1 cup hazelnuts, toasted
1⅓ cups superfine sugar
5 egg whites
pinch of cream of tartar
4 cups coffee ice cream
FOR THE CHOCOLATE CREAM
2 cups whipping cream
10 ounces semisweet chocolate, melted
*   and cooled*
2 tbsp coffee liqueur
white chocolate curls and fresh
*   raspberries, to decorate*

1 ▲ Preheat the oven to 350°F. Line three baking sheets with non-stick baking paper, then, using a plate as a guide, mark an 8 inch circle on each sheet and turn the paper over. In a food processor fitted with the metal blade, process the hazelnuts until chopped. Add a third of the sugar and process until finely ground.

2 In a clean grease-free bowl, whisk the egg whites until frothy, then add the cream of tartar and whisk until they form soft peaks. Gradually sprinkle the sugar over the whites, 2 tbsp at a time, whisking until the whites are stiff and glossy, then fold in the nut mixture. Divide the meringue among the baking sheets and spread out within the marked circles. Bake for 1 hour until firm and dry. Let cool in the turned-off oven, then peel off the paper.

3 ▼ Let the ice cream stand for 15–20 minutes in a large bowl and then beat with an electric mixer until smooth. Spread half of the ice cream over one meringue layer, top with a second meringue layer and spread with the remaining ice cream. Place the last meringue layer on top, press down gently, then wrap and freeze for at least 4 hours until firm.

4 ▲ To make the chocolate cream, beat the whipping cream until soft peaks form. Quickly fold in the cooled melted chocolate and the liqueur. Take the meringue cake out of the freezer, unwrap and place on a serving plate. Spread the chocolate cream over the top and sides of the meringue and return to the freezer. Wrap when firm. To serve, let the meringue stand for 15 minutes at room temperature to soften slightly before cutting.

MERINGUES WITH CHESTNUT CREAM   *Petits Mont Blancs*

This dessert takes its name from the famous peak in the French Alps, Mont Blanc, as the meringues piled high with chestnut purée and whipped cream resemble it.

SERVES 6

2 egg whites
pinch of cream of tartar
½ cup superfine sugar
½ tsp vanilla extract
chocolate shavings, to decorate
FOR THE CHESTNUT CREAM
⅓ cup superfine sugar
½ cup water
1 pound can unsweetened chestnut purée
1 tsp vanilla extract
1½ cups heavy cream
FOR THE CHOCOLATE SAUCE
8 ounces semisweet chocolate, chopped
¾ cup heavy cream
2 tbsp rum or brandy (optional)

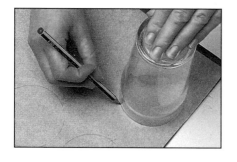

1 ▲ Preheat the oven to 275°F. Line a baking sheet with non-stick baking paper. Use a small plate to outline six 3½ inch circles and turn the paper over (so the meringue does not touch the pencil marks).

2 In a clean greasefree bowl, using an electric mixer, beat the egg whites slowly until frothy. Add the cream of tartar, then increase the speed and continue beating until they form soft peaks. Gradually sprinkle over the sugar, 2 tbsp at a time, and continue beating until the whites are stiff and glossy. Beat in the vanilla extract.

3 ▲ Spoon the whisked egg whites into a large pastry bag fitted with a medium-size plain or star nozzle and pipe six spirals following the outlines on the marked paper. Bake for about 1 hour until the meringues feel firm and crisp, lowering the oven temperature if they begin to brown. Using a thin spatula, transfer the meringues to a wire rack to cool completely.

4 ▲ To make the chestnut cream, place the sugar and water in a small saucepan over medium-high heat and bring to a boil, stirring until the sugar dissolves. Boil for about 5 minutes, then remove the pan from the heat and set aside to cool. Put the chestnut purée in a food processor fitted with the metal blade and process until smooth. With the machine running, slowly add the sugar syrup in a thin stream until the chestnut purée is soft, but still holds its shape (you may not need all the syrup). Add the vanilla extract and process again then spoon into a medium bowl.

5 ▲ In another bowl, with an electric mixer, whisk the cream until soft peaks form, then add a spoonful to the chestnut cream and pulse to combine. Chill the remaining whipped cream.

6 ▲ Spoon the chestnut cream into a pastry bag fitted with a large star nozzle. Pipe a mound of chestnut cream in a swirl onto each meringue then pipe or spoon the remaining cream on top of the chestnut cream to resemble a mountain peak. Chill until ready to serve.

7 To make the chocolate sauce, heat the chocolate and cream in a small saucepan over medium-low heat, stirring frequently. Remove the pan from the heat and stir in the rum or brandy, if using. Set aside to cool, stirring occasionally. (Do not chill or the sauce will set.)

8 To serve, place each meringue on a plate and sprinkle with chocolate shavings. Serve the chocolate sauce separately.

CRÊPES WITH ORANGE SAUCE

Crêpes Suzette

This is one of the best known French desserts and is easy to do at home. You can make the crêpes in advance; then you will be able to put the dish together quickly at the last minute.

SERVES 6

⅔ cup flour
¼ tsp salt
2 tbsp superfine sugar
2 eggs, lightly beaten
1 cup milk
4 tbsp water
2 tbsp orange flower water or orange
    liqueur (optional)
2 tbsp unsalted butter, melted, plus more
    for frying

FOR THE ORANGE SAUCE
6 tbsp unsalted butter
¼ cup superfine sugar
grated zest and juice of 1 large orange
grated zest and juice of 1 lemon
⅔ cup fresh orange juice
4 tbsp orange liqueur, plus more for
    flaming (optional)
brandy, for flaming (optional)
orange segments, to decorate

1 ▲ In a medium bowl, sift together the flour, salt and sugar. Make a well in the center and pour in the beaten eggs. Using an electric whisk, beat the eggs, adding a little flour until it is all incorporated. Slowly whisk in the milk and water to make a smooth batter. Whisk in the orange flower water or liqueur, if using, then strain the batter into a large pitcher and set aside for 20–30 minutes. If the batter thickens, add a little milk or water to thin.

2 ▲ Heat a 7–8 inch crêpe pan (preferably nonstick) over medium heat. Stir the melted butter into the crêpe batter. Brush the hot pan with a little extra melted butter and pour in about 2 tbsp of the batter. Quickly tilt and rotate the pan to cover the base with a thin layer of batter. Cook for about 1 minute until the top is set and the base is golden. With a spatula, lift the edge to check the color, then carefully turn over the crêpe and cook for 20–30 seconds, just to set. Slide the crêpe out onto a plate.

3 ▲ Continue cooking the crêpes, stirring the batter occasionally and brushing the pan with a little melted butter as and when necessary. Place a sheet of wax paper between each crêpe as they are stacked to prevent sticking. (Crêpes can be prepared ahead to this point – wrap and chill until ready to use.)

4 To make the sauce, melt the butter in a large frying pan over medium-low heat, then stir in the sugar, orange and lemon zest and juice, the additional orange juice and the orange liqueur.

5 ▲ Place a crêpe in the pan browned-side down, swirling gently to coat with the sauce. Fold it in half, then in half again to form a triangle and push to the side of the pan. Continue heating and folding the crêpes until all are warm and covered with the sauce.

6 ▲ To flame the crêpes, heat 2–3 tbsp each of orange liqueur and brandy in a small saucepan over medium heat. Remove the pan from the heat, carefully ignite the liquid with a match then gently pour over the crêpes. Scatter over the orange segments and serve at once.

ALSATIAN PLUM TART

Tarte aux Prunes Alsacienne

Fruit and custard tarts, similar to a fruit quiche, are typical in Alsace. Sometimes they have a yeast dough base instead of pastry. You can use other seasonal fruits in this tart, or a mixture of fruit.

SERVES 6–8

1 pound ripe plums, halved and pitted
2 tbsp Kirsch or plum brandy
¾ pound shortcrust or sweet shortcrust
    pastry
2 tbsp seedless raspberry jam
FOR THE CUSTARD FILLING
2 eggs
¼ cup superfine sugar
¾ cup heavy cream
grated rind of ½ lemon
¼ tsp vanilla extract

COOK'S TIP

If you have time, chill the
pastry shell for 10–15 minutes
before baking.

---

1 ▼ Preheat the oven to 400°F. Mix the prepared plums with the Kirsch or plum brandy and set aside for about ½ hour.

2 Roll out the pastry thinly and use to line a 9 inch pie pan. Prick the base of the pastry shell all over and line with foil. Add a layer of baking beans and bake for 15 minutes until slightly dry and set. Remove the foil and the baking beans.

3 ▲ Brush the base of the pastry shell with a thin layer of jam, then bake for 5 minutes more. Remove the pastry shell from the oven and transfer to a wire rack. Reduce the oven temperature to 350°F.

4 ▲ To make the custard filling, beat the eggs and sugar until well combined, then beat in the cream, lemon rind, vanilla extract and any juice from the plums.

5 ▲ Arrange the plums, cut side down, in the pastry shell and pour over the custard mixtur . Bake for about 30–35 minutes until a knife inserted in the center comes out clean. Serve the tart warm or at room temperature.

UPSIDE-DOWN APPLE TART   *Tarte Tatin*

This tart was first made by two sisters who served it in their restaurant near Sologne in the Loire Valley. A special tarte tatin *pan is ideal, but an ovenproof frying pan will do very well.*

SERVES 8–10

½ pound puff or shortcrust pastry
10–12 large Golden Delicious apples
lemon juice
½ cup butter, cut into pieces
½ cup superfine sugar
½ tsp ground cinnamon
crème fraîche or whipped cream, to serve

1 On a lightly floured surface, roll out the pastry into an 11 inch round less than ¼ inch thick. Transfer to a lightly floured baking sheet and chill.

2 Peel the apples, cut them in half lengthwise and core. Sprinkle the apples generously with lemon juice.

3 ▲ In a 10 inch *tarte tatin* pan, cook the butter, sugar and cinnamon over medium heat until the butter has melted and sugar dissolved, stirring occasionally. Continue cooking for 6–8 minutes, until the mixture turns a medium caramel color, then remove the pan from the heat and arrange the apple halves, standing on their edges, in the tin, fitting them in tightly since they shrink during cooking.

4 Return the apple-filled pan to the heat and bring to a simmer over a medium heat for 20–25 minutes until the apples are tender and colored. Remove the pan from the heat and cool slightly.

5 ▼ Preheat the oven to 450°F. Place the pastry on top of the apple-filled pan and tuck the edges of the pastry inside the edge of the pan around the apples. Pierce the pastry in two or three places, then bake for 25–30 minutes until the pastry is golden and the filling is bubbling. Let the tart cool in the pan for 10–15 minutes.

6 To serve, run a sharp knife around edge of the pan to loosen the pastry. Cover with a serving plate and, holding them tightly, carefully invert the pan and plate together (do this carefully, preferably over the sink in case any caramel drips). Lift off the tin and loosen any apples that stick with a spatula. Serve the tart warm with cream.

COOK'S TIP

If you do not have a heavy ovenproof pan, use a deep, straight-sided frying pan. If the handle is not ovenproof, wrap well in several layers of strong foil to protect it from the heat.

CHOCOLATE CLASSICS

Everyone loves chocolate. The French have a
way with chocolate – from airy chocolate
mousse to dense chocolate cake, from velvety
smooth chocolate sorbet to rich, round
chocolate truffles, it is the quintessential finish
to a memorable meal. In fact, it is hard to
imagine a sensational dinner party without
a chocolate component, at least a little
something with the coffee. The recipes in
this chapter reveal the secrets of
French chocolate creations.

CHOCOLATE MOUSSE CAKE *Gâteau Mousse au Chocolat*

This special occasion dessert is a double batch of chocolate mousse, glazed with chocolate ganache and decorated with long, slim chocolate curls – heaven for chocolate lovers!

SERVES 8–10

10 ounces semisweet chocolate, chopped
½ cup unsalted butter, cut into pieces
8 eggs, separated
¼ tsp cream of tartar
3 tbsp brandy or rum (optional)
chocolate curls, to decorate
FOR THE CHOCOLATE GANACHE
1 cup heavy cream
8 ounces semisweet chocolate, chopped
2 tbsp brandy or rum (optional)
2 tbsp unsalted butter, softened

1 Preheat the oven to 350°F. Lightly butter two 8–9 inch springform pans or loose-based cake pans and line the bases with buttered wax paper or nonstick baking paper.

2 ▲ In a saucepan, melt the chocolate and butter over low heat until smooth, stirring frequently. Remove the pan from the heat and whisk in the egg yolks until completely blended. Beat in the brandy or rum, if using, and pour into a large bowl. Set aside, stirring occasionally.

3 In a clean greasefree bowl, using an electric mixer, beat the egg whites slowly until frothy. Add the cream of tartar, increase the speed and continue beating until they form soft peaks, then stiffer peaks that just flop over a little at the top.

4 Stir a large spoonful of white into the chocolate mixture to lighten it, then fold in the remaining white until they are just combined (a few white streaks do not matter).

5 ▲ Divide about two-thirds of the mousse between the two prepared pans, smoothing the tops evenly, and tap gently to release any air bubbles. Chill remaining mousse.

6 Bake for 30–35 minutes until puffed; the cakes will fall slightly. Cool on a wire rack for 15 minutes, then remove the sides of the pans and let cool completely. Invert the cakes on to the rack, remove the cake pan bases and peel off the papers. Wash the cake pans.

7 ▲ To assemble the cake, place one layer, flat side down in one of the clean pans. Spread the remaining mousse over the surface, smoothing the top. Top with the second cake layer, flat side up. Press down gently so the mousse is evenly distributed. Chill for 2–4 hours or overnight.

8 ▲ To make the *ganache*, bring the cream to a boil in a heavy saucepan over medium-high heat. Remove the pan from the heat and add the chocolate all at once, stirring until melted and smooth. Stir in the brandy or rum, if using, and beat in the softened butter. Set aside for about 5 minutes to thicken slightly (*ganache* should coat the back of a spoon in a thick smooth layer).

9 ▲ Run a knife around the edge of the assembled cake to loosen it, then remove the sides of the pan. Invert the cake onto a wire rack, remove the base and place the rack over a baking sheet. Pour the warm *ganache* over the cake all at once, tilting gently to help spread it evenly on all surfaces. Use a spatula to smooth sides, decorate the top with chocolate curls, then allow to set.

RICH CHOCOLATE CAKE

Tarte au Chocolat

This dark, fudgy cake is easy to make, stores well and is a chocolate lover's dream come true.

SERVES 14–16

9 ounces semisweet chocolate, chopped
1 cup unsalted butter, cut into pieces
5 eggs
½ cup superfine sugar, plus 1 tbsp and
*   some for sprinkling*
1 tbsp cocoa powder
2 tsp vanilla extract
cocoa powder, for dusting
chocolate shavings, to decorate

1 Preheat the oven to 325°F. Lightly butter a 9 inch springform pan and line the base with nonstick baking paper. Butter the paper and sprinkle with a little sugar, then tap out the excess sugar from the pan.

2 ▲ The cake is baked in a *bain-marie*, so carefully wrap the base and sides of the pan with a double thickness of foil to prevent water from leaking into the cake.

3 Melt the chocolate and butter in a saucepan over low heat until smooth, stirring frequently, then remove from the heat. Beat the eggs and ½ cup of the sugar with an electric mixer for 1 minute.

4 ▲ Mix together the cocoa and the remaining 1 tbsp sugar and beat into the egg mixture until well blended. Beat in the vanilla extract, then slowly beat in the melted chocolate until well blended. Pour the mixture into the prepared pan and tap gently to release any air bubbles.

5 ▲ Place the cake pan in a roasting tin and pour in boiling water to come ¾ inch up the side of the wrapped pan. Bake for 45–50 minutes until the edge of the cake is set and the center still soft (a skewer inserted 2 inches from the edge should come out clean). Lift the pan out of the water and remove the foil. Place the cake on a wire rack, remove the side of the pan and let the cake cool completely (the cake will sink a little in the center).

6 Invert the cake onto the wire rack. Remove the base of the pan and the paper. Dust the cake liberally with cocoa and arrange the chocolate shavings around the edge. Slide the cake onto a serving plate.

CHOCOLATE SORBET

Sorbet au Chocolat

This velvety smooth sorbet has long been popular in France. Unsweetened chocolate gives by far the richest flavor, but if you can't track this down, then use the very best quality dark Continental plain chocolate that you can find or the sorbet will be too sweet.

<u>SERVES 6</u>

5 ounces unsweetened chocolate, chopped
4 ounces plain chocolate, chopped
1 cup superfine sugar
2 cups water
chocolate curls, to decorate

1 ▲ Put all the chocolate in a food processor, fitted with the metal blade and process for 20–30 seconds until finely chopped.

2 ▲ In a pan over medium-high heat, bring the sugar and water to a boil, stirring until the sugar dissolves. Boil for about 2 minutes, then remove from the heat.

3 ▼ With the machine running, pour the hot syrup over the chocolate. Allow the machine to continue running for 1–2 minutes until the chocolate is completely melted and the mixture is smooth, scraping down the bowl once.

4 ▲ Strain the chocolate mixture into a large measuring cup or bowl, and leave to cool, then chill, stirring occasionally. Freeze the mixture in an ice cream machine, following the manufacturer's instructions or see Cook's Tip (left). Allow the sorbet to soften for 5–10 minutes at room temperature and serve in scoops, decorated with chocolate curls.

COOK'S TIP

If you don't have an ice cream machine, freeze the sorbet until firm around the edges. Process until smooth, then freeze again.

85

QUEEN OF SHEBA CAKE

Gâteau Reine de Saba

This rich chocolate and almond cake is so moist it needs no filling. It is wonderful for entertaining as it can be made in advance and stored, well wrapped, in the refrigerator. for up to three days.

SERVES 8–10

⅔ cup whole blanched almonds, lightly toasted
⅔ cup superfine sugar
¼ cup flour
½ cup unsalted butter, softened
5 ounces semisweet chocolate, melted
3 eggs, separated
2 tbsp almond liqueur (optional)
FOR THE CHOCOLATE GLAZE
¾ cup heavy cream
8 ounces semisweet chocolate, chopped
2 tbsp unsalted butter
2 tbsp almond liqueur (optional)
chopped toasted almonds, to decorate

1 ▲ Preheat the oven to 350°F. Lightly butter an 8–9 inch springform pan or deep loose-based cake pan. Line the base with nonstick baking paper and dust the pan lightly with flour.

2 In the bowl of a food processor fitted with the metal blade, process the almonds and 2 tbsp of the sugar until very fine. Transfer to a bowl and sift over the flour. Stir to mix then set aside.

3 ▲ In a medium bowl, beat the butter with an electric mixer until creamy, then add half of the remaining sugar and beat for about 1–2 minutes until very light and creamy. Gradually beat in the melted chocolate until well blended, then add the egg yolks one at a time, beating well after each addition, and beat in the liqueur, if using.

4 ▲ In another bowl, beat the egg whites until soft peaks form. Add the remaining sugar and beat until the whites are stiff and glossy, but not dry. Fold a quarter of the whites into the chocolate mixture to lighten it, then alternately fold in the almond mixture and the remaining whites in three batches. Spoon the mixture into the prepared pan and spread evenly. Tap the pan gently to release any air bubbles.

5 Bake for 30–35 minutes until the edge is puffed but the center is still soft and wobbly (a skewer inserted about 2 inches from the edge should come out clean). Transfer the cake in its pan to a wire rack to cool for about 15 minutes, then remove the sides of the cake pan and let cool completely. Invert the cake onto an 8 inch cake board and remove the base of the pan and the paper.

6 To make the chocolate glaze, bring the cream to a boil in a saucepan. Remove from the heat and add the chocolate. Stir gently until the chocolate has melted and is smooth, then beat in the butter and liqueur, if using. Cool for about 20–30 minutes until slightly thickened, stirring occasionally.

7 ▲ Place the cake on a wire rack over a baking sheet and pour over the warm chocolate glaze to cover the top completely. Using a spatula, smooth the glaze around the sides of the cake. Spoon a little of the glaze into a pastry bag fitted with a writing nozzle and use to write a name, if you like. Let stand for 5 minutes to set slightly, then carefully press the nuts onto the sides of the cake. Using two long spatulas, transfer the cake to a serving plate and chill until ready to serve.

BITTER CHOCOLATE MOUSSE

Mousse au Chocolat Amer

This is the quintessential French dessert – easy to prepare ahead, rich and extremely delicious. Use the darkest chocolate you can find for the best and most intense chocolate flavor.

SERVES 8

8 ounces semisweet chocolate, chopped
4 tbsp water
2 tbsp orange liqueur or brandy
2 tbsp unsalted butter, cut into small pieces
4 eggs, separated
6 tbsp heavy cream
¼ tsp cream of tartar
3 tbsp superfine sugar
crème fraîche or sour cream and chocolate curls, to decorate

COOK'S TIP

As the flavor of this dessert depends on the quality of the chocolate used, it is worth searching in specialty shops for really good chocolate, such as Valrhona and Lindt Excellence.

---

1 Place the chocolate and water in a heavy saucepan. Melt over low heat, stirring until smooth. Remove the pan from the heat and whisk in the liqueur and butter.

2 ▲ With an electric mixer, beat the egg yolks for 2–3 minutes until thick and creamy, then slowly beat into the melted chocolate until well blended. Set aside.

3 ▲ Whip the cream until soft peaks form and stir a spoonful into the chocolate mixture to lighten it. Fold in the remaining cream.

4 In a clean greasefree bowl, using an electric mixer, beat the egg whites slowly until frothy. Add the cream of tartar, increase the speed and continue beating until they form soft peaks. Gradually sprinkle over the sugar and continue beating until the whites are stiff and glossy.

5 ▲ Using a rubber spatula or large metal spoon, stir a quarter of the egg whites into the chocolate mixture, then gently fold in the remaining whites, cutting down to the bottom, along the sides and up to the top in a semicircular motion until they are just combined. (Don't worry about a few white streaks.) Gently spoon into an 8 cup dish or into eight individual dishes. Chill for at least 2 hours until set and chilled.

6 Spoon a little crème fraîche or sour cream over the mousse and decorate with chocolate curls.

CHOCOLATE TRUFFLES   *Truffes au Chocolat*

These truffles, like the prized fungi they resemble, are a Christmas speciality in France. They can be rolled in cocoa or nuts, or dipped in chocolate – use plain, milk or even white chocolate.

<u>MAKES 20–30</u>

¾ cup heavy cream
10 ounces semisweet chocolate, chopped
2 tbsp unsalted butter, cut into pieces
2–3 tbsp brandy (optional)
FOR THE COATING
cocoa
finely chopped pistachio nuts or
*   hazelnuts*
14 ounces semisweet, milk or white
*   chocolate or a mixture*

1 ▲ In a saucepan over medium heat, bring the cream to a boil. Remove from the heat and add the chocolate, then stir until melted and smooth. Stir in the butter and the brandy, if using, then strain into a bowl and leave to cool. Cover and chill for 6–8 hours or overnight.

2 ▲ Line a large baking sheet with wax paper. Using a small ice cream scoop or two teaspoons, form the chocolate mixture into 20–30 balls and place on the paper. Chill if the mixture becomes soft.

3 ▲ To coat the truffles with cocoa, sift the cocoa into a small bowl, drop in the truffles, one at a time, and roll to coat well, keeping the round shape. To coat with nuts, roll truffles in finely chopped nuts. Chill well wrapped, for up to 10 days.

4 To coat with chocolate, freeze the truffles for at least 1 hour. In a small bowl, melt the dark, milk or white chocolate over a pan of barely simmering water, stirring until melted and smooth, then allow to cool slightly.

5 Using a fork, dip the frozen truffles into the cooled chocolate, one at a time, tapping the fork on the edge of the bowl to shake off the excess. Place on a baking sheet lined with nonstick baking paper and chill at once. If the melted chocolate thickens, reheat until smooth. Wrap and store as for nut-coated truffles.

BASIC RECIPES

This section includes essential basic recipes for French cooking – flavorful stocks for soups and stews, classic savory and sweet sauces and perfect pastries – all you need to get started.

HOMEMADE STOCKS

Homemade stocks are best for sauces and stews, and if you need to reduce them, the sodium will be lower than with storebought broth which tends to be high in sodium. Homemade stock is very easy to make, and cooks itself.

Meat Stock
Fond de viande

MAKES 12 CUPS

8–10 pounds raw or cooked beef or veal bones and meat and/or poultry carcasses, clean trimmings and giblets
2 large unpeeled onions, halved and root end trimmed
2 medium carrots, peeled and cut in large pieces
1 large celery stalk, cut in large pieces
2 leeks, cut in large pieces
1 or 2 parsnips, cut in large pieces
2–4 garlic cloves
large bouquet garni
1 tbsp black peppercorns

Place all the ingredients in a large stock pot and cover with cold water by at least 1 inch. Bring to a boil over medium heat. As the liquid heats, foam will begin to appear on the surface. Begin skimming off the foam with a large spoon or ladle as soon as it appears, continuing until it stops surfacing; this will take at least

5 minutes and by then the stock will be boiling. Reduce the heat until the stock is just simmering and simmer very slowly, uncovered, for 4–5 hours, skimming occasionally. Do not allow the stock to boil again or cover it as this can cause the stock to sour or cloud.

Top up with a little boiling water during cooking if the liquid level falls below the bones and vegetables.

Ladle the stock into a large bowl; discard the bones and vegetables. Leave the stock to cool, then chill to allow any fat to solidify, then scrape off the fat. To remove any further traces of fat, "wipe" a piece of paper towel across the surface. The stock can be used as it is or, if you wish, reduced to concentrate the flavor and chilled or frozen.

Brown Stock
Fond brun

Brown stock has a rich flavor and deep color, obtained by browning the meats and vegetables before cooking. Place the meat and vegetables in a large roasting tin and brown in the oven at 450°F for 30–40 minutes, turning occasionally. Put ingredients in the stockpot with the bouquet garni and proceed as for Meat Stock.

Chicken Stock
Fond de volaille

MAKES 8 CUPS

4½ pounds raw chicken carcasses, necks or feet or cooked carcasses
2 large onions, unpeeled, halved and root end trimmed
3 carrots, peeled and cut in large pieces
1 celery stalk, cut in large pieces
1 leek, cut in large pieces
2 garlic cloves, unpeeled and lightly smashed
1 large bouquet garni

Proceed as for Meat Stock, but simmer for 2 hours.

Brown Chicken Stock
Fond de volaille brun

Brown the chicken pieces in a frying pan, as roasting is too intense and the chicken could easily burn. Put the ingredients in the stockpot with the bouquet garni and proceed as for Chicken Stock.

Game Stock
Fond de gibier

Proceed as for Chicken Stock using game carcasses, with or without browning as described.

Fish Stock
Fumet de poisson

MAKES 8 CUPS
*2 pounds heads and bones and trimmings
    from white flesh
1 onion, thinly sliced
1 carrot, thinly sliced
1 leek, thinly sliced
8 parsley stems
½ bay leaf
1 cup dry white wine
1 tsp black peppercorns*

Put all the ingredients in a large non-reactive saucepan or flameproof casserole and add enough cold water to cover. Bring to a boil over medium-high heat, skimming any foam which rises to the top. Simmer gently for 25 minutes; strain through a cheesecloth-lined strainer. Cool, then chill. Reduce, if you wish, for storage or freezing.

COOK'S TIP

Make stock whenever you roast a piece of meat on the bone or a bird, or save bones and carcasses in the freezer until you have enough for a large pot of stock. After making stock, reduce it by at least half and freeze in an ice cube tray. Store the cubes in a strong freezer bag and add to soups and sauces without defrosting. Never add salt to the stock as it will be concentrated during reduction and always season sauces after adding the stock.

BASIC SAVORY SAUCES

There is a huge repertoire of sauces in classic French cuisine, but many are variations of a few types which you can master with a little practice. Sauces are usually categorized by the way they are made.

REDUCTION SAUCES
These are simply the cooking juices, sometimes with additional liquid such as wine, stock and/or cream, boiled to concentrate the flavor and thicken by evaporation.

FLOUR-BASED SAUCES
This type of sauce is usually thickened with cooked butter and flour (*roux*) and they are among the most useful for the home cook. They can be made with milk for *béchamel* or stock for *velouté* sauce, are sometimes enriched with cream and may also be flavored with other ingredients such as cheese, mushrooms, spices, mustard or tomato.

Sometimes the cooking liquid of soups and stews is thickened with flour, either by flouring the ingredients before browning them or by sprinkling over the flour during cooking. Alternatively, a flour and butter paste, known as *beurre manié*, may be stirred in at the end of cooking to thicken the liquid. Other flours, such as cornstarch, potato flour or arrowroot, may also be used for thickening sauces.

EMULSIFIED SAUCES
Hollandaise, *Béarnaise* and butter sauces, are included in this group. These sauces are very quick to make, but can be tricky to prepare and keep warm. The most common cause of the sauce separating or curdling is overheating. Mayonnaise is also an emulsified sauce and all the ingredients should be at room temperature for best results.

FLAVORED BUTTERS
These "hard" sauces, butter flavored with herbs or garlic, are useful to have on hand to give a lift to plain vegetables or sautéed or broiled meat, poultry or fish. An even simpler flavored butter, *beurre noisette*, is made by heating butter until it turns nutty brown before pouring over food.

VEGETABLE SAUCES
Sauces may also be thickened with vegetable purées, using, for instance, the aromatic vegetables cooked with a stew. Or a vegetable purée may be the sauce itself, for instance, fresh tomato sauce.

White Sauce
Béchamel

MAKES ABOUT 1 CUP
*2 tbsp butter
3 tbsp flour
1 cup milk
1 bay leaf
freshly grated nutmeg
salt and freshly ground black pepper*

Melt the butter in a heavy saucepan over a medium heat, add the flour and cook until just golden, stirring occasionally. Pour in half the milk, stirring vigorously until smooth, then stir in the remaining milk and add the bay leaf. Season with salt, pepper and nutmeg, then reduce the heat to medium-low, cover and simmer gently for about 5 minutes, stirring occasionally.

Velouté Sauce

Proceed as for White Sauce above, using stock or cooking liquid instead of milk.

Hollandaise Sauce

SERVES 6
¾ cup unsalted butter, cut
*   into pieces*
3 egg yolks
1 tbsp cold water
1–2 tbsp fresh lemon juice
½ tsp salt
cayenne pepper

Clarify the butter by melting it in a small saucepan over a low heat; do not boil. Skim off any foam.

In a small heavy saucepan or in the top of a double boiler, combine the egg yolks, water, 1 tbsp of the lemon juice, and salt and pepper and whisk for 1 minute. Place the saucepan over a very low heat or place the double boiler top over barely simmering water and whisk constantly until the egg yolk mixture begins to thicken and the whisk begins to leave tracks on the base of the pan; remove from heat.

Whisk in the clarified butter, drop by drop until the sauce begins to thicken, then pour in the butter a little more quickly, making sure the butter is absorbed before adding more. When you reach the milky solids at the bottom of the clarified butter, stop pouring. Season to taste with salt and cayenne and a little more lemon juice if wished.

Béarnaise Sauce

Combine 2 tbsp each tarragon vinegar and dry white wine with 1 finely chopped shallot in a small heavy saucepan, set over a high heat and boil to reduce until the liquid has almost evaporated. Remove from the heat and leave to cool slightly. Proceed as for Hollandaise Sauce, but omit the lemon juice and add the egg yolks to the shallot mixture. Strain before serving if you prefer.

Butter Sauce
Beurre blanc

SERVES 4–6
2 shallots, finely chopped
6 tbsp white wine vinegar
1 tbsp light cream
¾ cup unsalted butter, cut into
*   12 pieces*
salt and white pepper

Put the shallots and vinegar in a small heavy saucepan. Boil over a high heat until the liquid has almost evaporated, leaving only about 1 tbsp. Stir in the cream. Reduce the heat to medium and add the butter, one piece at a time, whisking constantly until it melts before adding the next (lift the pan from the heat if the butter melts faster than it can be incorporated). Strain the sauce and adjust the seasoning before serving.

COOK'S TIP

Delicate sauces, such as Béarnaise, Hollandaise and Butter Sauce, are easy to keep warm in a wide-mouthed thermos flask.

Mayonnaise

MAKES ABOUT ½ CUP
2 egg yolks
1 tbsp Dijon mustard
1 cup extra virgin olive oil
lemon juice or white wine vinegar
salt and white pepper

Combine the egg yolks and mustard in a small bowl. Beat for 30 seconds until creamy. Beat in the olive oil drop by drop until the mixture begins to thicken, then add the remaining oil in a thin stream until the mixture is thick. Thin the mayonnaise with a little lemon juice or vinegar, and season to taste. Store in the fridge for up to 2 days.

BASIC SWEET SAUCES

Custard Sauce
Crème Anglaise

SERVES 4–6
1 vanilla bean
2½ cups milk
8 egg yolks
¼ cup granulated sugar

Split the vanilla bean lengthwise and scrape the tiny black seeds into a saucepan. Add the milk and bring just to a boil, stirring frequently. Remove from the heat, cover and let stand for 15–20 minutes.

Whisk the egg yolks and sugar for 2–3 minutes until thick. Whisk in the hot milk and return the mixture to the saucepan.

With a wooden spoon, stir over a medium-low heat until the sauce begins to thicken and coat the back of the spoon (do not allow to boil or the custard may curdle). Immediately strain the sauce into a chilled bowl and let cool, stirring occasionally, then chill.

Fruit Sauce
Coulis de Fruit

MAKES 1¼ CUPS
1 pound fresh fruit, such as raspberries, strawberries, mangoes, peaches and kiwi fruit
1 tbsp lemon juice
2–3 tbsp superfine sugar
2–3 tbsp fruit brandy or liqueur (optional)

Put the fruit, lemon juice and sugar in a food processor fitted with the metal blade. Process for 1 minute, scraping down the sides once. Press the fruit purée through a fine sieve into a small bowl, stir in the brandy or liqueur, if using, and chill for 1–2 hours until cold.

Chocolate Sauce
Sauce Chocolat

MAKES ⅔ CUP
3 ounces semisweet or Continental chocolate, chopped
6 tbsp heavy cream
1–2 tbsp brandy or liqueur

In a small saucepan, bring the cream to a boil, then remove from the heat. Add the chocolate all at once and stir gently until melted and smooth. Stir in the brandy or liqueur, pour into a sauceboat and keep warm until ready to serve.

FRENCH PASTRY

French pastry has a firm, compact texture, much like shortbread, yet it is extremely light and crisp.

To make pastry the French use a special low-gluten flour. All-purpose flour produces good results, but better still, use a special cake and pastry flour, or use imported French flour which can be found in speciality shops, or look for low-gluten flour in health food shops.

Unsalted butter produces a crisp texture but, for a more tender result, substitute one part vegetable shortening to three parts butter.

Pastry, especially *pâte sucrée*, can be flavoured with vanilla extract, ground cinnamon, brandy or a liqueur, and ground almonds or hazelnuts can be substituted for part of the flour.

When using a food processor, be careful not to overwork the pastry.

Shortcrust Pastry
Pâte Brisée

Pâte brisée, which means "broken dough", is a versatile basic shortcrust pastry. The ingredients are "broken together" or rubbed in. After the liquid is added, it is kneaded by a process called *fresage*, where the heel of one hand is used to blend the ingredients into a soft pliable dough.

Pâte brisée is suitable for pies, quiches, tarts and tartlets. For sweet recipes a little sugar may be added which gives the pastry extra color and crispness.

FOR A 9–10 INCH PIE OR TART OR TEN 3 INCH TARTLETS
1¼ cups flour, plus more if needed
½ tsp salt
1 tsp superfine sugar (optional)
½ cup unsalted butter, cut into small pieces
3–8 tbsp iced water

In a large bowl, sift together the flour, salt and sugar, if using. Add the butter and rub in using your fingertips, until fine crumbs form. Alternatively, whizz the ingredients in a food processor.

Slowly add the water, mixing until a crumbly dough begins to form; do not overwork the dough or it will be tough. Pinch a piece of dough: it should hold together. If the dough is crumbly add a little more water. If it is wet and sticky, sprinkle over a little more flour.

Turn the dough on to a piece of plastic wrap. Hold the plastic wrap with one hand and use your other hand to push the dough away from you until the dough is smooth and pliable. Flatten the dough to a round and wrap in the plastic wrap. Chill for 2 hours or overnight. Leave to soften for 10 minutes at room temperature before rolling out.

To line a pie pan: lightly butter a 9–10in loose-based pie pan. On a lightly floured surface, roll out the dough to a thickness of about ⅛in. Gently roll the pastry loosely around the rolling pan, then unroll over the pie pan and gently ease the pastry into the pan, leaving a 1in overhang.

With floured fingers, press the overhang down slightly toward the base of the pan to reinforce the side; roll the rolling pin over the rim to cut off the excess. Press the pastry against the side of the pan to form a rim slightly higher than the side of the pan. If you like, crimp the edge. Prick the base with a fork and chill for at least 1 hour.

Quick Puff Pastry
Pâte demi-feuilletée

Puff pastry, *pâte feuilletée*, is tricky and time-consuming to make – this quick and easy pastry gives a similar feather-light result.

MAKES 1¼ POUNDS
⅞ cup cold unsalted butter
1½ cups cake or pastry flour
¼ tsp salt
½ cup cold water

Cut the butter into 14 pieces and place in the freezer for 30 minutes, or until very firm.

Put the flour and salt into a food processor and pulse to combine. Add the butter and pulse three or four times; there should still be large lumps of butter. Run the machine for 5 seconds while pouring the water through the feed tube, then stop the machine. The dough should look curdy. Tip the mixture on to a lightly floured, cool work surface and gather into a flat ball – you should still be able to see pieces of butter. If the butter is soft, chill the dough for 30 minutes or longer.

Roll out the dough on a floured surface to a 16 × 6 inch rectangle. Fold in thirds, bringing one end down to cover the middle, then fold the other end over it, like folding a letter. Roll out again to a long rectangle and fold again the same way. Chill the dough for at least 30 minutes.

Roll and fold twice more, then chill and fold the dough, well wrapped, for at least 30 minutes, or for up to 3 days, before using.

COOK'S TIP

The richer the pastry dough, the harder it is to handle. However, if rolling the dough becomes too difficult, simply press it into the pan with your hands, patching any cracks or holes with extra dough.

Rich Shortcrust Pastry
Pâte Sucrée

Pâte sucré, sweet pastry, is a type of *pâte brisée* with sugar and egg yolks added. Sugar makes the dough more crumbly, or "sandy" and in fact it is often called *pâte sablée*, or "sandy pastry". It is somewhat difficult to handle, but is especially delicious for fruit tarts.

FOR A 9–10 INCH TART OR TEN
3 INCH TARTLETS
1 cup flour, plus more if
*   needed*
½ tsp salt
3–4 tbsp confectioner's sugar
½ cup unsalted butter, cut into small
*   pieces*
2 egg yolks beaten with 2 tbsp
*   iced water and ½ tsp vanilla*
*   extract (optional)*

In a food processor fitted with the metal blade, process the flour, salt, sugar and butter for 15–20 seconds, until fine crumbs form. Remove the cover and pour in the beaten egg yolk and water mixture. Pulse the machine just until the dough begins to stick together. Do not allow the dough to form a ball or the pastry will be tough. If the dough appears dry, add a little water and pulse until the dough just holds together. Turn the dough onto a piece of plastic wrap and, holding the plastic with one hand, use your other hand to push the dough away from you until it is smooth and pliable. Flatten the dough into a round and wrap in the plastic. Chill for at least 2 hours.

GLOSSARY

The following terms are frequently used in French cooking. In the recipes we have tried to reduce the use of technical terms by describing the procedures, but understanding these words is helpful.

BAIN-MARIE: a baking pan or dish set in a roasting pan or saucepan of water. It allows the food to cook indirectly and protects delicate foods; a double boiler is also a kind of water bath, or *bain-marie*.

BAKE BLIND: to bake or part-bake a pastry shell before adding a filling, usually done to prevent the filling making the pastry soggy.

BASTE: to moisten food with fat or cooking juices while it is cooking.

BEURRE MANIÉ: equal parts of butter and flour blended to a paste and whisked into simmering cooking liquid for thickening after cooking is completed.

BLANCH: to immerse vegetables and sometimes fruit in boiling water in order to loosen skin, remove bitterness or saltiness or preserve color.

BOIL: to keep liquid at a temperature producing bubbles that break the surface.

BOUQUET GARNI: a bunch of herbs, usually including a bay leaf, thyme sprigs and parsley stalks, used to impart flavor during cooking, often tied for easy removal.

CLARIFY: to make an opaque liquid clear and remove impurities; stocks are clarified using egg white, butter by skimming.

COULIS: a purée, usually fruit or vegetable, sometimes sweetened or flavored with herbs, but not thickened, used as a sauce.

CROÛTONS: small crisp pieces of fried or baked crustless bread.

DEGLAZE: to dissolve the sediment from the bottom of a cooking pan by adding liquid and bringing to a boil, stirring. This is then used as the basis for a sauce or gravy.

DEGREASE: to remove fat from cooking liquid, either by spooning off after it has risen to the top or by chilling until the fat is congealed and lifting it off.

DICE: to cut food into square uniform pieces about ¼in.

EMULSIFY: to combine two usually incompatible ingredients until smooth by mixing rapidly while slowly adding one to the other so they are held in suspension.

FOLD: to combine ingredients, using a large rubber spatula or metal spoon, by cutting down through the center of the bowl, then along the side and up to the top in a semicircular motion; it is important not to deflate or over-work ingredients while folding.

FOOD MILL *(mouli-légumes)*: tool for puréeing found in most French kitchens which strains as it purées.

GLAZE: to coat food with a sweet or savory mixture producing a shiny surface when set.

GRATINÉ: to give a browned, crisp surface to a baked dish.

HERBES DE PROVENCE: a mixture of aromatic dried herbs, which grow wild in Provence, usually thyme, marjoram, oregano and summer savory.

INFUSE: to extract flavor by steeping in hot liquid.

JULIENNE: thin matchstick pieces of vegetables, fruit or other food.

MACERATE: to bathe fruit in liquid to soften and flavor it.

PAPILLOTE: a greased non-stick baking paper or foil parcel, traditionally heart-shaped, enclosing food for cooking.

PARBOIL: to partially cook food by boiling.

POACH: to cook food, submerged in liquid, by gentle simmering.

REDUCE: to boil a liquid for the purpose of concentrating the flavor by evaporation.

ROUX: a cooked mixture of fat and flour used to thicken liquids such as soups, stews and sauces.

SAUTÉ: to fry quickly in a small amount of fat over a high heat.

SCALD: to heat liquid, usually milk, until bubbles begin to form around the edge.

SCORE: to make shallow incisions to aid penetration of heat or liquid or for decoration.

SIMMER: to keep a liquid at just below boiling point so the liquid just trembles.

SKIM: to remove froth or scum from the surface of stocks etc.

STEAM: moist heat cooking method by which vaporized liquid cooks food in a closed container.

SWEAT: to cook gently in fat, covered, so liquid in ingredients is rendered to steam them.

INDEX